Our Sacred Source

Our Sacred Source

A Theology Grounded in Modern Physics, about a Creator God and Why We Are Here

ANDREW KNEIER

WIPF & STOCK · Eugene, Oregon

OUR SACRED SOURCE

A Theology Grounded in Modern Physics, about a Creator God and Why We Are Here

Copyright © 2021 Andrew Kneier. All rights reserved. Except for brief quotations in critical publications or reviews, no part of this book may be reproduced in any manner without prior written permission from the publisher. Write: Permissions, Wipf and Stock Publishers, 199 W. 8th Ave., Suite 3, Eugene, OR 97401.

Copyright obtained 08–10–20 from the US Copyright Office
Case No. 1–9111293151

Wipf & Stock
An Imprint of Wipf and Stock Publishers
199 W. 8th Ave., Suite 3
Eugene, OR 97401

www.wipfandstock.com

PAPERBACK ISBN: 978-1-7252-8825-6
HARDCOVER ISBN: 978-1-7252-8826-3
EBOOK ISBN: 978-1-7252-8827-0

01/04/21

To the Memory of Paul Tillich

Contents

Acknowledgments		ix
Introduction		1
1	The Book of Nature	13
2	God's Purposes	35
3	God's Purposes in Relation to Goodness, Beauty, and Love	45
4	On Having a Purposeful Life	63
5	The Theology of Paul Tillich: God as the Ground of Our Being	73
6	A Personal God?	86
7	The Experience of God's Presence	95
8	God and the Problem of Evil	106
9	A Theology of Death	116
10	A Theology of the Human Spirit	134
Bibliography		147

Acknowledgments

I COULD LIST HERE the countless professors of religion and theology that have shaped my thought about God and about the human condition. I would start with my years as a member of the Christian Brothers, a Catholic order of male educators. From there I would move to my professors at the University of San Francisco, a Jesuit institution where I completed a major and masters degree in theology. Then it was on to the University of Chicago Divinity School. I was working on my doctorate there when a cancer diagnosis and the guidance of a therapist in dealing with it caused me to switch gears. I then obtained my doctorate in clinical psychology with the aim of helping patients with cancer as I had been helped. Here I encountered other professors who shaped my thought about the suffering that afflicts us all, to varying degrees, and about the resources in our minds to help us. Then I worked with cancer patients at the University of California, San Francisco, Comprehensive Cancer Center for nearly three decades. The professors and physicians there helped me appreciate the endless ways people suffer with cancer. The hundreds of patients I worked with revealed to me firsthand the perils of our bodily existence. We need a theology to help with this; that was my thought then, and that's what I hope is offered in this book.

All the professors and clinicians in these institutions shaped the thought that went into this book. I owe this book to their education, influence, and guidance.

If you look at my bibliography you will find all of the physicists, philosophers, and theologians who together have created a mountain of insight for me, and for all of us, I believe, and I like to think I stand on their shoulders. I want to mention Isaac Newton and Albert Einstein especially, as they believed their discoveries about the created world revealed aspects of the Creator's nature, purposes, and mind.

Many family members, friends, and colleagues offered helpful suggestions on my manuscript. I am indebted most especially to my older brother Gary, a former monk and currently a clinical psychologist and mystic. He read the entire manuscript from the first page to the last, offering unbroken encouragement and theological insight.

When I ask myself, why do I think what I think and believe what I believe, I can take no credit because the wisdom of so many others has poured into me and given rise to this book.

Introduction

[*A note on usage. In this book, I use the word "God" to refer, most generally, to the deity who created our world. There is a danger in doing this because most people have preconceived ideas about God that could undermine the fresh, open-minded, start-from-the-beginning approach that I take in addressing the question of God's nature and His purposes. Sometimes I will refer to God as the Creator or Creator Deity. When I am referring specifically to the God of the Bible, the context will make that clear. I will also follow the convention of referring to God as a "He," even though it seems odd to apply a human gender to a creator deity. Also, I will follow the custom of capitalizing He and Himself when referring to God.*]

THIS BOOK IS AN original work of theology, so I start by saying what I think that means and how it might speak to us personally. Theology is telling a story about God.[1] I am calling it a story because we cannot prove it to be factual, and because stories use plots, analogies, and metaphors to convey meaning, and this is also true of the theology presented here. And while it cannot be proved, it beckons to be believed and taken to heart. It speaks to the truth of our existence, that we are here for a purpose; and it speaks to that truth in ways that are scientifically and philosophically sound. And if we accept it as true, it can become true *for us*. It can enlighten us, inspire us, move us. That is the hope that guides the theology of this book.

---

1. This point was repeatedly made by Karen Armstrong in her popular book *The History of God*. Her book is the history of the *idea* of God and *stories* about God in Christianity, Judaism, and Islam.

Theology is not only about God. It is also about us and about our humanness. The wondrous aspects of our humanness are mixed with aspects that are troubling for most of us. The challenges life throws at us can seem relentless and unforgiving. Just by being human we are doomed to suffer, each in our own way. Our suffering can have a perverse power over us, causing us to lose sight of all the ways we've been blessed.

But we have power too, as seen in the amazing resilience we find in ourselves when we are battered by life. There is power in our enduring capacity for gratitude for everything good that has happened to us and for every gift of love we have received. Life can be astoundingly joyful in countless ways. In this book's theology there is a sacred source to the power that beats within us, the power to embrace life on its own terms, in spite of our suffering. The source of this power is God's spirit in our innermost depth.

This theology speaks to both the positive and negative aspects of our humanness, helping us understand how and why they came about. On the positive side, it aims to help us grasp and celebrate the sheer wonder of life. And yet it can also help us master its many downsides—the heartaches, the illnesses, the injuries, the impairments, the obstacles, all the myriad ways we can suffer.

I mentioned aspects of being human that can be considered troubling, and I've chosen to touch on just nine of those below. I believe we all know of these troublesome aspects, but I want to mention them here so we can be on the same page when it comes to the problems of our existence the theology of this book aims to address. If we ask ourselves, what is it like to be a human being, a truthful answer is not a rosy picture. I believe it is important to call a spade a spade when it comes to the ways our humanness can harm and encumber us. And I believe we need a theology to rescue us from a sense of melancholy and resignation about the state of our being, and a theology to help us master the challenges we face. Without such a theology we might just shrug, thinking: Oh well, I guess we are stuck in a meaningless and sorrowful existence. *But in this book's theology, we are not stuck.*

Some Troubling Aspects of Our Humanness

1. *Our Human Nature*

We find ourselves having a nature that imperils us, making us vulnerable to devastating injuries and illnesses. We have no control over many of the bad things that can happen to us. Our bodies make the human condition intrinsically unsafe. Our minds can make it troubling and confusing, for we don't choose to have most of the thoughts we have. They come to us unbidden. Oftentimes, the physical and mental suffering that afflict us comes out of the blue, not caused by us and not resulting from our failure to protect ourselves. As we all know, bad things can happen to good people, so our being good provides no protection.

We are both the victims and beneficiaries of circumstances beyond our control. We need the power to move from victim to victor and the grace to cherish and be grateful for all the ways life has been good to us.

2. Having to Die

We are mortal because we are human, and even if we accept our mortality, we still live in the quiet fear of what dying will be like. Our mortality also undermines our quest for meaning because everything we do with our lives will amount to nothing in the long run. Nothing can last forever. This applies to us too; eventually we will be lost and forgotten after we die. A day will come when no one will remember us, when there will be no remnant of our having existed. And a day will come when our planet will perish, along with the human race it produced.

I am not sure we can fully grasp what it means to cease to exist when our bodies die. And having to die confronts us with losses we cannot fully fathom. How can we bring ourselves to say goodbye to life, to everything about life that we love, and to the people we love as well. And how can we tolerate the loss they will experience, as they have to say their final goodbyes to us.

3. The Pressure of Life

Because time is limited, we live under pressure to make the most of it while we can. Only by denying this fact can we fully relax, as if we had all the time in the world to accomplish our goals. There is also the pressure of living up to our ideals, which most of us fail to do. And there's the pressure of being on schedule, when it comes to accomplishing what we want to accomplish in life, and experiencing what we want to experience. It is common for people to feel they are behind schedule, and that they need to get going, lest their dreams of personal fulfillment fall away. There is definitely pressure in this.

4. We Live in Mystery

Our existence confronts us with all the things we cannot possibly know.[2] And many of the things we cannot possibly know go to the heart of our existence. By some means we came to be.[3] This we know and feel in our bones. And yet *how* we came to be, our ultimate causes, are shrouded in mystery. Because we cannot know these causes, we cannot know the full truth of our existence, of what we truly are.

How we came to be is part of how the universe came to be. And yet the ultimate origin of the universe is one of those things we cannot possibly know, just as our true origins remain a secret. It doesn't help to say the universe was caused by the big bang or that we were created through evolution. Science cannot say with certainty how the big bang happened because the laws of physics cannot reach that far back. And evolution was built upon everything that existed before life started, and yet science cannot penetrate the ultimate nature of the matter and forces that allowed life to evolve.

The theologian Reinhold Niebuhr wrote about the mystery of our existence in his appropriately-titled classic *On the Nature and Destiny of Man*.[4] His bottom line was that faith was needed to penetrate these mysteries because they lie beyond the wisdom of science and reason.

5. The Loneliness of Our Existence

Our inner life and the nonstop talking we do to ourselves cannot be fully known by another person. We live in a private cocoon. Because of this, no one can know us as we know ourselves. No one can fully grasp what it is like to be us. It works the other way too, as we cannot penetrate the inner life of another person or fully grasp what it is like to be them. What's more, no one can know our suffering as we experience it, just as we cannot appreciate another person's suffering as they experience it. We each die our own individual death. Finally, we can know about the suffering of large masses of our fellow humans, and yet carry on with our daily lives as if we didn't know it.

---

2. Collins, "Within Any Possible Universe."

3. This is how the distinguished German theologian Friedrich Schleiermacher expressed the basis for religious faith. *Christian Faith*, 13.

4. Niebuhr, *Nature and Destiny of Man*, vol. 1, *Human Nature*.

6. The Givenness of Life

We find ourselves being who and what we are. These are the givens of our existence. Our bodies and minds feel given to us. We are *created* creatures, created by realities and forces not of our own making. These realities are ultimately in charge; we certainly did not fashion our own existence. There is something mysterious about the givenness of our lives. It can make us wonder about an intelligence or structure in the universe that determines what's given.

7. Our Lives Seem Not to Matter

We want our lives to matter, to make a lasting positive difference, somewhere, somehow. And yet there seems to be no such thing as a *lasting* positive difference. We can have an impact on the lives of our loved ones and even in making the world a better place. But our loved ones will eventually perish and even the world itself and all of mankind will not last. As I wrote above, there will come a day when no one will remember us and when there will be no remnant of our having existed. Who among us can deny the troubling question: what will it even matter that we lived?

8. Our Essential Smallness

The immensity of the universe and our unfathomable smallness in relation to it can make us feel insignificant and overshadowed. We can wonder about our place in it, how we fit in, how we count. Our smallness is not only in size; the time allotted to us is also tiny, in relation to the vast span of time in the cosmos. Because we are part of the universe, we would like to feel we belong here, that this is our home. But it can be hard to feel at home or that we count in a universe this immense; it makes our existence a tiny blip, a tiny atom in the deep ocean of time and space.

9. Why Are We Here?

We find ourselves being here, and we feel put here by a force or reality larger than us. It's natural to wonder *why*, whether there is a reason or purpose behind it. It can be argued that the human race was not planned, that we are the mindless by-product of evolution. But can anyone really be at peace with that, in their heart of hearts? Don't we reject the notion that we are an accident with no overarching purpose? And so we ask: Why are we here?

If we have the courage to face up to things the way they are, then we must contend with these realities and questions. This is why Robert Frost wrote we are all living lives of quiet desperation. The quandaries we inevitably confront cry out to us for answers and for some perspective to help us master them. This cry, from the depth of our being, cannot be silenced. The science behind our existence cannot tell us why we matter. Nor can it say our life here is all we have, that there is not something more that gives a reason and purpose behind it.

It is my belief that we need a robust and well-grounded theology to address the issues I have identified, and that is the reason for this book. In this book's theology, each human life has a purpose that we can regard as good and worthwhile, perhaps even sacred.

Physics says that everything is caused by something that came before it, that a chain of causality rules the physical world. This chain ultimately goes back to creation itself, and this is where theology enters in. Theology does not give a science behind the creation; rather, it offers an explanation, a story if you will, pertaining to its ultimate source. This source is believed to be a creator deity. (Henceforth I will refer to this deity as God.) Theology also addresses God's purposes in creating the universe and how these purposes apply to us. And it addresses where God lives now, after launching the creation, and the sense in which God's spirit is in us and can be a resource for us as we navigate through life and contend with challenges we inevitably encounter.

The theology presented in this book also addresses our wanting to feel we belong in this universe, despite our essential smallness as described above. We are not so small or insignificant in light of the common origin we share with the universe at large. It sprang from a seed that imbued it with certain ingredients, forces, and laws of nature, and these exist in us as well and count for what we are and how we came to be here. We came from the same source and we are made of the same stuff.

A Top-Down vs. A Bottom-Up Theology

Many theologies can be considered *top-down* because they start with a transcendent God, the existence and purposes of which are thought to be revealed in the inspired texts of various religions. They begin with an almighty God who is perfect and infinite in all His attributes, and go from there to the world He created and to us.

A *bottom-up* theology, as presented in this book, begins with the created world and looks there for clues to God's nature and purposes. It is based on the book of nature as opposed to a book created by humans or a book believed to be inspired by God and passed down to us. The book of nature is the starting point for this book's theology.

In a top-down theology, God is up there and we are down here. This God transcends us in every way imaginable. In a bottom-up theology, God is in the *depth*, in the deepest innermost part of creation. Everything is grounded in God. We are grounded in God as well. We find God in our innermost being, not up there in a transcendent realm.

The book of nature I am referring to describes the fundamental building blocks of matter and the fundamental forces in the natural world as revealed in contemporary physics. This is where I believe we need to look for clues about a Creator Deity. I believe this perspective reveals a God whose spirit lives in every speck and spark of the universe, and whose spirit abides in the innermost depth of our being.

When physicists probe into the fundamental, non-reducible constituents of matter and energy, they find themselves at a loss to explain why the ultimate foundations of nature are the way they are.[5] They are simply *given*, as facts of nature. Within and behind these facts, we find the God that is at the center of this book's theology. He is found within the foundations of our world. These foundations, I believe, have emanated from God's nature and reveal aspects of that nature. And His nature explains why things are the way they are. Nature and God are intertwined in the sense that the foundations of nature reveal God, and this God, in turn, explains why nature is the way it is.

This Book's Theology: A Chapter-by-Chapter Summary

Because I am telling a story about God, and about God's relation to us, I want to preview how this story unfolds, chapter by chapter.

Chapter 1: *The Book of Nature*

We start with the book of nature, as opposed to a revered religious text. The discoveries of modern physics about the fundamental building blocks and forces in nature have profound implications. This is the basis of this book's theology, as these discoveries could imply the existence of a creator God and aspects of His nature. This is the approach in much of natural theology, especially as seen in the theology of Isaac Newton and other deists in the

---

5. Greene, *Elegant Universe*, 10–13.

seventeenth century. When Newton was working out the law of gravitation, for example, he thought he was discovering a law put in nature by God and that revealed the orderliness of God's nature. That was long ago. Now, thanks to modern physics, we know so much more about the nature of matter and energy, and we can ask what these discoveries might reveal about God. Were Newton alive today, this would be his question. It would also be Albert Einstein's question, for he wanted to know the mind of God. I focus in chapter 1 on seven such discoveries and what they imply about God.

Chapter 2: *God's Purposes* and Chapter 3: *God's Purposes in Relation to Goodness, Beauty, and Love*

In these chapters we move on to the question of God's purposes in bringing the universe into being. Based on the twin ideas that the creation *emanated* from God and *manifests* aspects of His nature, we can imagine that God's essential goodness, beauty, and love are manifested in the created world. From these ideas, it is reasonable to speculate about His purposes—namely, that He created the world in order to promulgate His goodness, beauty, and love. And we actually find support for this speculation in modern physics, in the metaphysics of Plato and Alfred North Whitehead, and in the philosophy and neuroscience of love.

Chapter 4: *On Having a Purposeful Life*

In this chapter we turn to the question of how God's purposes apply to us and what it means to live a purposeful life. In this book's theology, all of creation is imbued with God's purposes as a driving force. And yet the fulfillment of His purposes is not a sure thing because of the random forces at work in the universe. Contemporary theoretical physics posit such forces, and in this book's theology, they account for the evil, ugliness, and hate in our world.

From this perspective, we have a better grasp on why we are here—namely, to manifest as much goodness, beauty, and love in our lives as we possibly can. This is how we are aligned with God's cause. This is how our lives honor God. The God within us is our ultimate resource in this regard. We are not alone in our quest for a purposeful and fulfilling life. We are empowered by our sacred source and the divinity in the ground of our being (our next chapter).

Chapter 5: *The Theology of Paul Tillich: God as the Ground of Being*

In chapter 5 we turn to the theology of Paul Tillich and his conception of God as the Ground of Being and thus as the Ground of Our Being. This conception is aligned with the God of this book's theology, although we base our theologies on different sources and conceptualize His nature in different ways. I see God as our most basic essence and base this on the discoveries of contemporary physics about the fundamental constituents of the natural world. Tillich's theology, on the other hand, is based on Judeo-Christian scriptures and existential philosophy. But we agree on an essential point: that the God within us is a resource for mastering the troubling aspects of our humanness and the slings and arrows of our misfortune. The idea that God is in us and can help us is fundamental to our theologies.

Chapter 6: *A Personal God?*

Is the God of this book's theology a person with whom we can have a personal relationship? And in what sense does God know and care about us? These questions will occupy us in chapter 6. While we may *want* a God who takes a personal interest in us, we still have to figure out, with sound theological concepts and methods, how the God who created the universe can also be a person-like being who resides in us, cares about us, and can help us, a God we might pray to, in other words. As I said in the first sentence of this introduction, my aim is to develop a theology that speaks to us personally. That's what this chapter intends to do.

Chapter 7: *The Experience of God's Presence*

Here we take on a challenge to this book's conception of God: if God resides in the innermost core of our being, then why don't we experience the presence of this God on a daily basis? Why aren't we always aware of the God within? We will explore three answers in this chapter. The first originated with Saint Augustine, who believed God was just too deep within us, too deep for us to reach or touch with our conscious minds.

A second answer is that God is alive within us in countless ways, even if we do not believe in God (whether the God of this book's theology or the God of religion). He is alive in us whenever we cherish being loved or when we act in loving and selfless ways. He moves us in our resilience in dealing with the challenges life inevitably entails. He is alive within us when we are grasped by the wonder of what we have, as opposed to being preoccupied by what we do not have. Our deep and insightful intuition is often given by God. We are seldom aware, however, that our inner God moves us in these ways.

A third answer is that many people do experience the personal presence of God in powerful and transforming ways. I turn to William James's classic study *The Varieties of Religious Experience* for documentation and analysis of such experiences.

Chapter 8: *God and the Problem of Evil*

For many, the problem of evil is perhaps the most resolute nail in God's coffin, proving that He is dead or never existed. The evil things that can happen to us, and that *do* happen to us, are legendary. How could this state of affairs exist if God is all-powerful and all-loving? The answer in this book's theology challenges the entire theory of an all-powerful God and attributes the evil in our world to the random forces that exist in the universe. Our theology suggests that these forces came from God's nature but are not willed by Him.

Chapter 9: *A Theology of Death*

We now turn to the ever-present reality of death in God's world. All living beings eventually die. We need a theology of death to explain this, a theology that sees the ebb and flow of life as grounded in God's nature and purposes. This chapter also offers a perspective on how God, as conceived in this book, can help us as our death approaches. Because life springs from God, we can praise God and give thanks; and because death is ordained by God, we can humbly accept our demise, as the energy that sustains us flows back into the ocean of energy from which future life evolves. Life and death are both *of God*: God is the *source* of life and the source also of death. God is with us as we die, making a peaceful death possible.

Chapter 10: *A Theology of the Human Spirit*

While the previous chapter offered a theology of death, here I propose a theology of the human spirit. This is a theology about the human response to trauma, a response of astounding courage, resilience, and perseverance . . . often called, simply, the human spirit. The history of our species is replete with countless testimonials to this spirit, and we can't help but to be in awe of them. We are taken aback by what they reveal. When pushed to our limits, there is something in our nature that pushes back. In this book's theology, the *source* of the remarkable tenacity is deep within us, from the spirit of God that resides there, in our innermost depth.

There are many ways to describe the human spirit, but the truth of this spirit is best revealed in real-life examples. If we want to know what we are made of, we can dig here, in these examples, as they reveal our true substance and power. In this book's theology, they reveal our inner God, and yet there are many questions we need to explore here. What do these examples reveal about this God? What is the mission of this God? What does He want for us?

The relevance of this theology is that it speaks to us personally, as I mentioned above. I believe each chapter does that, and perhaps this last chapter is a fitting last word on that topic, as it presents illustrations of how the human spirit, empowered by God, can turn even extreme adversity into a personal triumph.

Who is This Book For?

The book is written in clear, easy-to-read, nontechnical prose for lay persons who do not have a background in theology but who are interested in questions related to God and religion. These include the theological implications of contemporary physics, the sacred meaning and purposes of our existence, the source and meaning of our spirituality, and coming to terms with suffering and death. At the same time, the book aims to be relevant to religious professionals and to students and professors in divinity schools and theological seminaries.

I imagine most of my readers fall into one of four categories. I think you will be able to place yourself in one of these categories without much trouble.

The first category are those of you who already believe in God (presumably the Judeo-Christian God) but do not feel sufficiently inspired by your faith and are therefore reading a book like this. The God that nature reveals to us may deepen or enhance your faith, and I hope He does. But for some, it may be difficult to accept this God, who is less perfect and less powerful than the God of your religion.

The nonbelievers among you make up the second category. If I could, I would ask you about the nature of this God you do not believe in, because chances are I would not believe in this God either. I suppose you are reading this book because you are curious and open-minded. Perhaps you *want* to believe in a God, or in something more, but you can't because the God of religion is just too far-fetched. Nonetheless, you haven't quite given up on the God idea. I like to think you are searching for a more believable God. I think you will like this book.

Many of you fall into a third category. You are on the fence between belief and nonbelief. Perhaps you feel pulled both ways. On one side is the lure of what religion could offer you, in the way of a connection to a community of shared faith or feeling personally connected to God. But the skeptical voice of your rational mind is on the other side. I hope this book will sway you a bit . . . not necessarily toward a particular religion, but toward a sense of how your purpose here is related to God's purpose.

Finally, I imagine that some of you are not particularly struggling with religion *per se* or with questions about God, but are rather seeking a more meaningful spirituality. I hope this book will speak to your quest; you may find that chapters 4, 5, 6, and 7 have a special resonance.

1

The Book of Nature

It is difficult to overestimate the significance of the intellectual shift that occurred in Europe during the seventeenth and eighteenth centuries.[1] The central issue concerned the *method* for knowing the truth, whether in the physical sciences, philosophy, or theology. In prior centuries, the truth was regarded as something revealed by the authority of tradition (all the way back to Aristotle's teachings about the workings of nature) or the teachings of the church. The truth was found in what was taught to be true by those in positions of authority to know the truth. If a farmer's crops failed, for example, he or she might go to the local priest to learn how the hand of God was behind the farmer's misfortune.

All that changed with the advent of the scientific method. Now the success or failure of crops was explained by *discovered* knowledge about the workings of nature. This was a radical, monumental shift in thinking. Nearly everything thought to be true, because of the received wisdom of past centuries, was now challenged. It was not so much the *content* of taken-for-granted knowledge that was at issue; the issue concerned the *method* by which this knowledge was derived.[2] The new paradigm could be sum-

---

1. Grayling, "Epoch of Human History."
2. Kors, *Birth of the Modern Mind*, 1–7.

marized as follows: We find ourselves in a world that is governed by laws, and these laws can be discovered through rational investigation and trial-and-error experiment.

This new approach was applied to knowledge about God. The *existence* of the Judeo-Christian God, or of a Creator Deity, was widely accepted throughout Europe. The issue concerned the nature and will of this God. How could that be known? The church had its own answer to that question, according to which scripture and tradition were regarded as *the* sources of knowledge about God. These were now rejected as being unscientific—not necessarily wrong, but based on an untenable method of discovery. The correct method, it was now believed, was to look at the created world, the world of nature, for insight into the nature and will of the creator. *This was because God's nature was manifested in the world He created.* This was the key point.

Isaac Newton is a good example. In 1687 he announced to the world that he had happened upon a law of God, a law put in nature by God to make the universe an orderly, lawful place. This was the universal law of gravitation, a law that Newton believed revealed the lawful orderliness of God's nature. Think about this for a moment. Newton discovered that any two bodies in the universe attract each other with a force that is directly proportional to the product of their masses and inversely proportional to the square of the distance between them. This fascinating law is *in nature*, but how did it get there? It would be farfetched to think it occurred by accident. He believed it came from God. In a sense, he was doing theology when he was doing his science. Nowadays, we would say he was doing "natural theology"; but even in his day, this concept was sometimes used to describe his work.

It was not only Newton who believed the creator God was revealed in His creation. Other giants of the scientific revolution shared the same belief, including Galileo, Copernicus, and Kepler. It gradually became a widespread belief among other scientists (or "natural philosophers," as they were called) and among the intellectual class at the time. Throughout European culture, the dominance of the church, whose teachings about God were based on Scripture, gave way to the new approach to learning about God—namely, through a scientific exploration of the book of nature.

If we jump forward to the beginning of the twentieth century we find Albert Einstein with similar beliefs. When asked whether he believed in God, he wrote: "My religiosity consists of a humble admiration of the infinitely superior spirit that reveals itself in the little we can comprehend about the knowable world. That deep emotional conviction in the presence of a superior reasoning power, which is revealed in the incomprehensible universe, forms my idea of God."³ In response to a student who asked about his religious faith, he said:

> Everyone who is seriously involved in the pursuit of science becomes convinced that a spirit is manifest in the laws of the Universe—a spirit vastly superior to that of man, and one in the face of which we with our modest powers must feel humble. In this way the pursuit of science leads to a religious feeling of a special sort, which is indeed quite different from the religiosity of someone more naïve.⁴

Thanks to Einstein and the burgeoning fields of particle physics and astrophysics, we now know much more about the book of nature than in the era when Newton made his discoveries. Since the time of Aristotle, it was believed that atoms were the fundamental building blocks of matter. But the last fifty years brought in the burgeoning field of particle physics and the discovery that atoms were composed of much smaller particles (protons, neutrons, and electrons) and that protons and neutrons were composed of still smaller bits of matter (quarks and leptons). In addition, particle physics identified the fundamental forces at work in the microscopic world.⁵

In physics, the laws and principles of this world are called quantum mechanics. "Quanta" refer to the indivisible units of matter or energy that make up the quantum world. Because these units behave and interact in a fluid, dynamic manner, the term "quantum *dynamics*" would be more appropriate. There is nothing "mechanical" going on in this realm. Nonetheless, I will stick with the term "quantum mechanics" in the following discussion.

As I mentioned in the Introduction, the theology of the book you are now reading belongs to the field of natural theology. Its basic premise is that the book of nature, which we now see as vastly more intricate and rich than we ever knew, is a source of revelation about the Creator Deity. To elaborate on this point, I should say a word about the two principles that inform my method.

The principle of emanation. I believe the fundamental building blocks and forces in the natural world *emanated* from God's nature as opposed to being designed by God. By "fundamental," I mean the indivisible and foundational particles and forces that are not made of anything else. The electron, for example, is considered a "fundamental particle" because there is nothing else within it. The universe emanated from God in the sense that

---

3. Isaacson, *Einstein*, 388.
4. Isaacson, *Einstein*, 388.
5. Pollock, *Particle Physics for Non-physicists*.

the foundations of the created world flowed automatically from God's nature in the instant God willed this to happen. God knew His nature, and He knew what would flow from it. He knew that it would give rise to the laws of physics and to the subsequent evolution of the universe.

The concept of divine emanation, as describing the process by which the universe came from God, has a long theological history. For example, the thirteenth-century Dominican theologian Dietrich of Freiberg, taught that the universe emanated from God and therefore bears a likeness to God.[6] The goodness of God "overflowed" in His creation, which represented an "outpouring" of God's nature.

The principle of manifestation. Because the basic foundations of the natural world emanated from God, they can be seen as manifestations of God's nature. This principle enables us to infer something about God on the basis of what we discover about the fundamental particles, forces, and interactions in the quantum world and on the basis of how the universe evolved once these quantum fundamentals took over.

The sun is a good example of both emanation and manifestation. The energy, heat, and light that *emanate* from the sun are *manifestations* of what is going on in the core of the sun, that is, a thermonuclear fusion reaction.[7] Using the laws of physics, and starting with what emanates from the sun, scientists have been able to understand what is going on in the sun's core.

These two principles, emanation and manifestation, are the basis for the natural theology presented in this book. I believe they constitute the most solid basis for any propositions or speculations about God's nature. They do not prove God's existence, of course. Rather, assuming the existence of a Creator Deity, they constitute the best way of approaching the questions of God's nature and purposes. I don't mean to be presumptuous in making this claim, and realize other natural theologians may take exception to it. Nonetheless, I wanted you, as my readers, to know the method and assumptions that inform the theology I am presenting here.

The book of nature, which we are now exploring, has many chapters and offers many individual topics I could focus on. It would take a very long list to delineate all the new discoveries and theories that are relevant to our task at hand—namely, to explore what they might reveal about a Creator Deity. I have chosen a relatively short list:

1. *The Big Bang.* According to the big bang theory of how the universe began, certain initial conditions (showing God's nature?) needed to

---

6. Fuhrer, "Dietrich of Freiberg," 8–10.
7. Galfard, *Universe in Your Hand*, 18–19.

be in place, after which the laws of physics took over in driving the evolution of the universe.

2. *The Strong Nuclear Force.* This force, which is part of the Standard Model of Particle Physics, binds protons and neutrons within the nucleus of every atom that exists.

3. *Quantum Field Theory.* Here we are introduced to the fundamental force fields that operate in the microscopic and macroscopic worlds, without which there would be no universe as we know it.

4. *The Equivalence of Mass and Energy.* Einstein's famous $E=mc^2$ states that mass and energy (which are clearly ubiquitous in the universe) are actually two aspects or manifestations of the same thing.

5. *Electric Charge.* The electric charge within atoms enables them to hold together, as the positively charged nucleus keeps the negatively charged electrons from flying off.

6. *Dark Matter and Dark Energy.* The universe consists of "dark matter" (dark because it is invisible) that keeps galaxies from flying apart and "dark energy" that accounts for the continued expansion of the universe.

7. *Determinism and Randomness.* Classical physics operates (and works in the macroscopic world) on the assumption of causal determinism, while quantum mechanics operates (and works in the microscope world) on the assumption of a fundamental randomness embedded in nature.

I will elaborate on each of these in the discussion that follows. For now, I want to be clear about my reasons for taking up these topics. I want to explore what they could reveal about God's nature, and I want to illustrate the method of speculative discourse that I am employing, a method that hinges on the twin principles of emanation and manifestation. I hope that other theological thinkers will use this method whenever they take up some fundamental aspect of the created world that science reveals to us. They could ask: What might these basic aspects of nature reveal (by inference) about God because they are manifestations of God's nature? Anyone asking such questions would be in the good company of Newton, Einstein, and countless others.

Seven Chapters in the Book of Nature

Let me return to the theme of this chapter, namely: What might the scientific discoveries about the natural world (over the last century) reveal about a creator God? Let's take up the examples I have chosen to focus on.

1. *The Big Bang.* The origin of the universe has always been a perplexing and daunting mystery for mankind, even though countless creation stories have evolved in various cultures and religions. These stories were always a matter of faith, not of rational or scientific knowledge.

Over the last forty years, however, cosmologists have traced the origin of the universe back to The Big Bang. Using the known laws of physics, they have been able to go back in time, through all the eons of the universe, until they ran up against a wall that pertained to the very first instant.[8] On their side of the wall, they were able to describe what took place in the big bang. It began when the universe was only a trillionth of a second old and involved an explosive expansion during which the universe exponentially doubled in size about one hundred times within the tiniest fraction of a second.[9] They call this expansion the big bang; more technically, it is called the cosmological inflation era.[10] Starting with the big bang, scientists have been able to explain the subsequent evolution of the universe using the laws of physics alone.[11]

On the other side of this wall were the *initial conditions* of our universe, the conditions that gave rise to the big bang. The period during which these conditions were in place is called the Planck Era (named after Mac Planck, the German physicist who originated the quantum theory). The conditions during the Planck Era are a matter of speculation and inference. That's the wall cosmologists are up against.[12] They can speculate about these conditions based on the aftermath of the big bang and the subsequent evolution of the universe; but ultimately, they are confronting a very vexing mystery.[13] In other words, cosmologists have not been able to answer the questions: What was it that exploded? What were the initial conditions that gave rise to the explosion? What was the state of the universe before the big bang kicked in?[14]

---

8. Singh, *Big Bang*, ch. 1, "In the Beginning," 3–83. Singh, *Big Bang*, 255. Rovelli, *Seven Brief Lessons on Physics*, 47.

9. Galfard, *Universe*, 49, 108. Greene, *Elegant Universe*, 345–47. Randall, *Knocking on Heaven's Door*, 352.

10. Singh, *Big Bang*, 477.

11. Tegmark, *Our Mathematical Universe*, 94.

12. Greene, *Elegant Universe*, 347, 356, fig. 14.1.

13. Randall, *Knocking on Heaven's Door*, 374.

14. Galfard, *Universe*, 49. Davies, *Mind of God*, 57, 89. Singh, *Big Bang*, 488–92.

Some theologians have argued that the big bang more or less proves the existence of the biblical God who created the universe,[15] while others have adopted the more conservative view that the big bang allows for a hypothesis about the existence of a creator God to answer the question, Where did the big bang come from?[16] I hold to this more conservative view. I can state it as a hypothesis, but it is also my belief: the initial conditions from which the universe emanated were the primordial manifestation of God's nature. Put differently, I believe God resided within the Planck Era and that back then, He only existed in that sliver of time.

I have referred to "God's nature" many times and should try to state more clearly what I mean by that. In science and philosophy, "nature" is that elusive, abstract essence that makes something what it is. It is an abstraction because if you were to dissect something down to its smallest parts, you would never find its "nature." When we ask, "What is human nature?" we are asking, "What is it that makes us human?" To answer this question, we would try to define the essence of a human being, that definitional something that makes us human. When we say someone has an aggressive nature, we are saying that aggression is an inherent part of that person's makeup.

When I write about God's *nature*, I am referring to those essential attributes that make God who He is. This is obviously a matter of speculation, but in this book, my speculation about God's nature is based on what the created world might reveal about God because this world, in its fundamental makeup, emanated from God's nature and is therefore a manifestation of that nature.

If you understand the method and approach I'm using, then you will grasp why I'd want to know what cosmologists have been able to extrapolate about this initial state, about the so-called Planck Era from which our universe arose and evolved.

First, in the initial instant of creation, all the mass/energy[17] in the universe was concentrated into a single point, a point of nearly infinite density that could not be further diluted.[18] This single, initial point of colossal density has been referred to as the "primeval atom."[19] In physics, density

---

15. Harris, *Analytic Philosophy of Religion*, 129.

16. For a review of these arguments, see Halvorson and Kraph, "Cosmology and Theology."

17. I am using the term "energy/mass" in light of Einstein's equation, $E=mc^2$, according to which energy can be converted to mass and mass into energy. For example, Randall, *Knocking*, 363, explains that the initial energy density was converted to matter as the early universe cooled.

18. Greene, *Elegant Universe*, 346, 350. Galfard, *Universe in Hand*, 99.

19. Singh, *Big Bang*, 159, 269.

refers to how much stuff is packed into a volume of space and how tightly packed it is. A pint of double rich chocolate ice cream is more dense than a pint of sorbet. The volume is the same (1 pint) but the atoms that make up the ice cream are more tightly packed than the atoms in the sorbet. The sorbet is therefore lighter and has more empty space between the atoms. Our universe began with a region of space so densely and tightly packed with energy/mass that nothing could be added. It was so compact that there was no empty or wasted space.

The density of the initial blob of substance, as it is sometimes called, was mostly uniform and smooth, but not perfectly so. If we scooped out some of our chocolate ice cream with a rubber spatula and then spread it on a flat plate, it would be mostly smooth because the molecules were tightly packed. Our sorbet would not be so smooth. There would be a kind of lumpiness due to ice crystals and bits of fruit. These could be called irregularities in the sorbet's density. Similarly, there were some irregularities (also called quantum fluctuations) in the density of our soon-to-be-born universe. Cosmologists believe these fluctuations in the Planck Era can be inferred from the cosmic structure (the distribution of galaxies and clouds of gas) that evolved from that era.[20] The initial fluctuations in density, in other words, essentially "seeded" this eventual, irregular distribution of matter in the universe.[21]

If we could expand our pint of sorbet to the size of the universe, we can imagine how the spaces between the ice crystals or bits of fruit, in the pint-size container, would be magnified in a universe of sorbet. Now we would find giant gaps between the crystals—gaps of several million light years. We could trace those back to our initial pint. This is essentially what our physicists have done in tracing back our universe's density irregularities (which are depicted in the background radiation from the big bang)[22] to the tiny irregularities that were present before the big bang. These tiny irregularities enabled the universe to evolve as it did. Had they not been present in the initial blob, then the universe that resulted from the inflationary instant would have been uniform and smooth, with no lumpiness in the distribution of matter that would allow galaxies to form. In other words, the structure and organization of the universe we can observe shows the imprinting of density irregularities in the initial state. That's the second thing we can extrapolate about the initial conditions of our universe. The density was not uniform.

---

20. Tegmark, *Our Mathematical Universe*, 66–67, 107–10. Galfard, *Universe in Hand*, 335.

21. Singh, *Big Bang*, 443, 477–78. Galfard, *Universe in Hand*, 364.

22. Randall, *Knocking*, 352–59. Greene, *Elegant Universe*, 349.

Because it was not uniform, a certain disorder also existed in the Planck Era. The orderliness of a system can be seen in how its parts fit together to create smoothly harmonious wholes free of chaotic disturbances. In physics, harmony and chaos are polar opposites. The Planck Era gave birth to a universe that was *mostly* ordered in this sense. Einstein, you will recall, was in awe of the intricate orderliness in the laws that governed the natural world. Our infant universe was not perfectly ordered, however. Because of its density irregularities (i.e., disorder) there was a bit of chaos in the initial conditions, and therefore the threat of chaotic consequences as these initial conditions expanded into our universe. That's the third thing we can extrapolate.

The basis for introducing the concepts of disorder and chaos, I believe, are found in the *randomness* at work in the way matter is distributed in the universe.[23] The initial conditions that gave rise to the big bang can be inferred from this element of randomness in the Plank Era. If we return to our pint of sorbet, a scoop of which we were to spread out on a flat plate, we would find no discernible pattern in the tiny spaces between the ice crystals or bits of fruit. These tiny spaces would appear to be *randomly* distributed. Similarly, the background radiation from the big bang, which depicts the initial Plank-era irregularities, shows no discernible pattern. The initial matter seemed to be scattered in a random manner. That's the forth thing we can extrapolate: random forces had a hand to play in the Planck Era.

Finally, there is the question of the immense heat that must have existed in the Planck Era. In physics, temperature normally refers to the movement of molecules within a given volume of space. When we heat water on the stove, the water molecules move faster and faster until they boil and begin to disperse or escape as steam. They are free to move about because the surface of the water is by and large unrestrained; the sides and bottom of the pot prevent the water molecules from going out to the side or down through the bottom. But at the surface, they are only restrained by atmospheric pressure. The Planck Era, however, is a different pot altogether. It is so dense that nothing can escape because there is nothing to escape into. All of space is concentrated there. In addition, there are no atoms or molecules there; those come later in the aftermath of the big bang. So what is moving around there to create heat? Because all the energy of our visible universe was concentrated at one point, the laws of physics break down when it comes to saying what the temperature of the Planck Era was or even what it was that was "hot."[24] Physicists have estimated that the temperature within

---

23. Tegmark, *Our Mathematical Universe*, 343–44.
24. Greene, *Elegant Universe*, 357. Singh, *Big Bang*, 489. Galfard, *Universe in Hand*, 99.

the big bang itself was 10^{32} degrees Celsius, but the temperature within the Planck Era could "soar to infinity."[25]

In order to know more about the initial state, we'd need a grand unified theory (covering the fundamental forces in the quantum world plus the workings of gravity in general relativity) and we'd need a way of testing the theory, which would require temperatures a million million times higher than experiments can presently reach. It is speculated that the densities and temperatures necessary to unify all the forces of nature only existed in the Planck Era.[26] Our only access to that era is theoretical and inferential.

Getting back to the theme of this chapter: What might the inferred initial conditions, as embodied in what we can hypothesize about the Planck Era, reveal about a Creator Deity? We are doing theology now, and maybe you can help answer this question. I can think of a few things.

The impenetrable density we've discussed suggests that the initial region of space was whole and complete unto itself. It could not be diluted or broken down to anything smaller. There were no subatomic particles such as quarks within it. Moreover, it consisted of all the space there was at the time; there was no space outside of this region. Nor was there any matter anywhere else.

Our working assumption is that this feature of the Planck Era is a manifestation of the Creator's nature—namely, that the Deity is whole and complete unto Himself. That's not much of a start, but it's something.

If we interject the notion of causality into the picture, we'd have to say this primordial, ultra-dense region of space was caused by itself. It had to be self-caused because there was nothing outside of it that could have caused it. We would add that it was also *self-sufficient*: nothing outside of it was necessary for it to exist since there was nothing outside of it.

Following our working assumption, the Creator would be self-sufficient and self-caused. "Goodie for the Creator!" you might exclaim. But seriously, can you think of anything else that is self-sufficient and self-caused? This certainly speaks to the stunning uniqueness of the Creator.

In metaphysics, the notion of Being refers to the fact that things are able *to be*, as opposed to being doomed to nonbeing. Moreover, things don't just exist, they are *being* what they are. Since Plato, philosophers have speculated about the source or ground of being—about that which enables things to be, and to be what they are. It is not enough to say, "Well, things just are." Philosophically, that would be an easy out, but it would eschew the question about the source. In the preceding paragraph, I said we could think of the

---

25. Greene, *Elegant Universe*, 357.
26. Randall, *Knocking*, 334–35.

Creator as being self-sufficient and self-caused. We can now elaborate on this by thinking of the Creator as being the source or ground of its own being. Could we say that about anything or anybody else?

The Creator was not only the source of its own being, of course; He was the source of *all* being because everything that ever existed emanated from Him. I am referring to what we have learned about the Planck Era, about that which exploded in the big bang, thereby creating the universe. Everything owes its *existence* to the Creator, but also its beingness is owed, that is, it being what it is with an intrinsic identity or essence. I don't mean the Creator specifically and intentionally created whole things, such as stars, planets, rocks, forms of life, etc. What was created were the elementary forces and particles that make up those things. This is what we have learned from cosmology and physics. The Planck Era gave rise to the fundamental particles and forces,[27] which in turn gave rise to everything else, obeying the laws of physics.

"No one has any explanation of why our universe is composed of these particular particles, with these particular masses and force charges.... The universe is the way it is because the matter and force particles have the properties they do."[28]

I grant that these speculations about the Creator have a positive spin. But if we stick to our method, adhering to the principles of emanation and manifestation, we'd also see some implied imperfections in the Creator's nature. By "imperfections," I mean there was not *perfect* uniformity or order in His nature. The density irregularities we have discussed imply elements of chaos and randomness in the Creator's nature. We might imagine the Creator, in knowing His nature, knew of certain discordant aspects.

For example, earlier we discussed the orderliness in the Planck Era, an orderliness that was manifested in the aftermath of the big bang, an orderliness that brought a harmonious working-together of parts to create viable, whole things. This is certainly true of every atom in the universe. Each one is made of many particles and forces, all which work together to create it.[29] In knowing Himself, the Creator would know of His orderliness, or perhaps of the forces that would create order in the world. But He could also apprehend something discordant within Himself, a bit of disorder or forces that could create disorder or chaos in the world.

Regarding the density irregularities, and their implications for chaos and randomness, it is tempting to think the Creator made these irregularities

---

27. Greene, *Elegant Universe*, 10–13.
28. Greene, *Elegant Universe*, 12–13.
29. Singh, *Big Bang*, 292–93, 329.

in order for the universe to have the structure it has, a structure that includes stars and galaxies, for example. This view implies that the Creator planned things out to be the way they are. As I've stated already, I believe it is more reasonable to see these irregularities as manifestations of the Creator's nature, a nature that the Creator found Himself having. If we stick to this idea, and follow the method we've employed, we would only conclude, for the time being, that the density irregularities reveal a lack of uniformity and some random forces within God's nature.

I cannot overemphasize the importance of this point with regard to the evil in the world. Presumably, God knew about the chaos and randomness in His nature and that things would not unfold perfectly in the universe that was to emanate from His nature. But He did it anyway, and (in my mind) there must have been a purpose behind it, which we discuss in the next chapter.

We have learned that the particles and forces within the Planck Era are considered fundamental and foundational for the subsequent evolution of the universe. I think we should keep this in mind as we explore the God revealed in the book of nature. We do not find God in a rock, for example. Nor do we find God in the atoms that make up the rock, for those atoms are not fundamental. What is fundamental are the particles and forces within the atoms, and those can be traced back to the big bang, even though we can only speculate inferentially on what it was that explored.

2. *The Strong Nuclear Force.* I mentioned earlier that atoms were thought to constitute the basic building blocks of matter until research into the microscopic world found a much more basic and smaller realm of particles and forces within atoms. Eventually these discoveries were consolidated in the Standard Model of Particle Physics.[30]

A central aspect of this model involves the Strong Nuclear Force, which binds neutrons and protons together in an atom's nucleus.[31] Neutrons and protons are comprised of smaller particles called quarks, and the strong force also binds those together. To execute this binding power, it employs force carriers call gluons, which can also be considered the smallest quanta of the strong force field.[32]

It is not known where the Strong Nuclear Force came from; it is just there, as a fact of nature. (Quantum Field Theory, discussed next, interprets this force as a manifestation of a force field.) It is the strongest force of nature

---

30. For a display of all the particles and forces in the standard model, see Randall, *Knocking*, 115.

31. Galfard, *Universe in Hand*, 191.

32. Galfard, *Universe in Hand*, 185. Greene, *Elegant Universe*, 416.

that we know of, and without it, the basic constituents of matter would fly apart and there would be no atoms, no anything.[33] But again, where did this essential, foundational force come from? This is where our Creator Deity might enter the picture.

The principles of interpretation that are guiding our exploration into the divine nature suggest that the Strong Nuclear Force flowed seamlessly from God's nature (as opposed to being designed by God for the purpose of keeping atomic nuclei together). This force is not literally God, in my view. Rather, it is *of God*, in the sense that it comes from God and is a manifestation of the bonding force that is an aspect of God's nature. We have all heard the expression, God is love. And yet what *is* love, if not a bond?[34] Thus, the idea that God is love could be a metaphor we have invented to capture the bonding aspect of God's nature. This bonding aspect is in every atom of every cell in our bodies.

Wherever atoms exist, there also is a manifestation of God's nature. This bonding force is not only *in* every atom, it enables every atom to exist and *to be* an atom. Here again we encounter the concept of being. When it comes to atoms, this force is the ground of their being.

In chapter 5, we will encounter Paul Tillich's theology about God as the Ground of Being. This metaphor, *ground*, is meant to capture the sense in which God is the *source* and *sustainer* of all being. The Strong Nuclear Force, as a manifestation of God's nature, is consistent with this idea. We might call it the *Glue* of Being instead of the Ground. This force that binds things together has a source. It comes from God. And it sustains the nucleus of every atom in the creation.

3. *Quantum Field Theory*. The notion that God is in everything and gives existence to all things can also be extrapolated from Quantum Field Theory, according to which the *fundamental* property of nature is found in the fields that permeate the entire universe.[35] That is a mouthful of a sentence, so I will break it apart and try to make sense of it.

When we think of fields, as far as physics is concerned, most of us will think of the magnetic field created by magnets or the gravitational field created by earth. But what exactly *is* a field? About the magnetic field, Einstein said that the "magnet calls into being something physically real in the space around it."[36] In Quantum Field Theory (QFT) this physically real thing is

---

33. Galfard, *Universe in Hand*, 186, 191.
34. I will elaborate on this notion in the next chapter, when discussing God's purposes.
35. Zee, *Quantum Field Theory in a Nutshell*, 3–6.
36. Einstein, *Out of My Later Years*, 71.

a property or condition of space itself. Space is not empty; it is permeated with fields that are physically real.[37] The entire universe is nothing but a beehive of various fields.

QFT is relevant to what we are trying to do here—namely, to see what quantum physics has discovered about the *fundamental* building blocks and forces in nature, and to ask what these might reveal about the Creator. In QFT, the fundamental reality of our world consists of fields (there are seven in all). In this view, subatomic particles are actually excited states or oscillations of a field, and the forces of nature (such as the Strong Nuclear Force considered above) are actually the activity of fields. It appears that the particles within the nucleus are tiny pieces of matter, but this is because the fields in question consist of discrete, indivisible, spread-out units. These units, or quanta, are the smallest possible amount of a field that can exist. In other words, when a particle physicist thinks he or she is seeing evidence of a particle, it is really a discrete unit of a field, of a property of space.

QFT gives us an *interpretation* of the nature of the fundamental forces and particles in the universe; whether this interpretation is accurate is a controversial topic among physicists. I want to give it the benefit of the doubt, for a moment, in order to comment on its theological implications. If we stick to the interpretative principles we have employed so far, then what emanated from the Creator was a scattering of fields and these fields (as the fundamental realities that underlie, inform, and permeate everything) can be regarded as *manifestations* of the Creator. The question before us would be: What aspect of God's nature do fields manifest?

One way of getting at this is to consider what fields actually *do*? Some are force fields, such as gravity and the electromagnetic field, because they exert forces.[38] Gravity exerts a pulling force on other objects, and the electric and magnetic fields that have a positive charge also exert a pulling or attractive force on negatively charged entities (recall what most of us learned in high school science, that "unlike charges attract"). We have already encountered the Strong Nuclear Force, which is the strong force field that binds protons and neutrons tightly together. So here again, in QFT, we see a bonding force that could reflect an aspect of God.

Perhaps more importantly, quantum fields are spread out through the entire universe and "link everything to everything."[39] All the matter and energy in the universe share a common foundational reality, that is, the fields from which they spring and which link them together. Instead

---

37. Brooks, *Fields of Color*, 6–10.
38. Brooks, *Fields of Color*, 16.
39. Galfard, *Universe in Hand*, 161, 23.

of saying everything exists *in* space, QFT says everything exists *of* space. That's because space is never empty; it is made up of quanta, of "atoms of space."[40] These quanta are the smallest units of a field that can exist and they can manifest themselves as particles or forces, which are constantly interacting. But they share a common foundation which links everything together, forming a network of relations that weaves the texture of space as an all-encompassing tapestry.[41]

In mysticism we come across the notion that "all is one" and that everything finds its common unity in God. QFT, insofar as we can interpret it as manifesting the bonding and unifying aspects of the Creator, is consistent with the mystical tradition.

But we have to be honest here and also note that, according to QFT, the pushing-apart forces that occur in nature are grounded in quantum fields. Thus, the repulsive force that two positively charged entities and two negatively charged entities have on each other ("like charges repel") reveal aspects of fields that oppose the binding or unifying aspects.

I should also mention the weak force field.[42] Insofar as it manifests aspects of God's nature, it is somewhat of a mixed bag. On the one hand, it has a destructive aspect in causing neutrons to decay. On the other hand, it initiates the nuclear fusion reaction within stars, without which the universe would be cold and dead. At the very least, this could mean that God is not one-dimensional (having only bonding aspects) and that the divine intentionality thought to drive the universe cannot be reduced to any one thing.

In addition to force fields, there are two matter fields that act on all known particles (one acts on particles called quarks and one acts on particles called leptons). Finally, the Higgs field is ubiquitous throughout the universe and is responsible for the mass that all particles have (the field imparts mass to particles as they pass through it, which all do).

QFT posits that fields are everywhere and do everything that needs to be done in order for our universe to exist. Most of the fields (but not all) can be seen as manifesting the bonding aspect of God's nature, a pulling together that enables our universe to be what it is. Before particles can bind, they also need to have mass, which is imparted as they pass through the so-called Higgs field. This is something else that needs to be done for our universe to be what it is. God's nature, as manifested in QFT, is taking care of business, in other words . . . and this business, essentially, is the *creation* of our world.

---

40. Rovelli, *Seven Lessons*, 43.
41. Rovelli, *Seven Lessons*, 43–44, 64.
42. Rovelli, *Seven Lessons*, 66–85.

4. *Electric Charge.* The mixture of creative and keeping-apart aspects of God can also be seen in the electric charges that pervade the universe. These charges originated with the universe, which initially consisted of a dense plasma of electrically charged particles, including wildly streaming electrons.[43] After a few hundred thousand years, the universe had cooled to a sufficient degree to allow these electrons to slow down enough to be captured by atomic nuclei, forming the first electrically neutral atoms (neutral because the protons in the nuclei were positively charged and electrons were negatively charged). Were it not for these charges, atoms would never have formed.[44]

The positive and negative charges between the nucleus and the electrons around it *attract* each other, which holds the atom together.[45] The force between them is called the electrostatic force. To say that the nucleus has a "positive" charge and electrons have a "negative" charge is arbitrary. What matters is how these charges interact, with like charges repelling each other and opposite charges attracting each other.

What exactly is a charge, however? We know it is a *fundamental property* of the constituents of matter (atomic nuclei and their electrons), but we don't really know what it is. We only know what it does. We can detect it in the electrostatic force it creates, but we don't know what is creating this force, except . . . well, the electric charge (a circular explanation). The question has also been posed, but not answered: Where does electric charge come from?[46]

It is clear there is something very creative in the interaction between positive and negative charges. There is a creative force that pulls opposite-charged particles together and thereby enables atoms to be. There is a consistent theme emerging here when it comes to the pulling-together or bonding aspect of God's nature (insofar as this nature is manifested in the electrostatic force).

But we also find something consistent with God's pushing-apart aspect, as seen in the repulsive interaction between like charges. If particles have the same charge, they are pushed apart and prevented from coming together. To give God the benefit of the doubt, perhaps the pushing-apart aspect in His nature belies a deep wisdom that particles with the same charge *need to be kept apart* because they are essentially incompatible. But why would these particles be incompatible if they have the *same* charge?

---

43. Greene, *Elegant Universe*, 347.
44. Randall, *Knocking on Heaven's Door*, 97.
45. Singh, *Big Bang*, 289, 292.
46. Galfard, *Universe in Hand*, 239–30.

Wouldn't their sameness make them intrinsically compatible? Perhaps not. Particles with the same charges could lack the *complementarity* that is seen in particles with opposite charges. What are we saying here? That the bonding aspect of God's nature, at least as manifested in the attraction of opposite charges, only operates when particles *are opposite* and can therefore complement each other? It would be a startling and deep conclusion to draw about the way bonding works in nature.

It would be tempting to say that God, in His wisdom, set things up this way. That God knew that particles with same charge needed to be kept apart because they did not complement each other. And that it was only the complementarity between unlike charges that caused their attraction. The idea that God set it up this way runs against the principle of emanation that we have established in our method. I would rather say, therefore, that the force of attraction based on complementarity was in God's nature, flowed out of God in the creation, and is now manifested in the behavior of charged particles.

It may also reflect something about God that electrical charges are always conserved.[47] This means that electric charge is an intrinsic, unalterable property of the particles that carry them. The bonds they create are fixed for good. The separation created by being alike is a serious matter.

We have positive and negative charges in every atom of ever cell in our bodies. It is not farfetched, therefore, to speculate on how these charges affect our human nature or how they shape our personal experience. The binding forces between opposite charges could give rise to the attachment dynamics in our own nature—that our attachments are based on a lack of sameness. Don't identical twins, for example, feel less attached to each other than fraternal twins? The pushing-apart forces between like charges could give rise to our tendency to maintain a certain distance from people who are too much like us. Such people do not complement us enough, and it may be *complementarity* that drives attachment.

5. *The Equivalence of Mass and Energy.* Let's go back to the Planck Era (see p. 5), which contained all the mass in the universe and all the energy as well. That's because mass and energy are exact manifestations of each other. Mass is a manifestation of energy just as energy is a manifestation of mass. This is based on Einstein's well-established equation $E=mc^2$. Mass can be converted to energy and energy can be converted to mass. But the conversion or exchange rate is far from equal. Einstein's equation establishes that a tiny amount of mass can be converted into a huge amount of energy.[48] Be-

---

47. Tegmark, *Our Mathematical Universe*, 164.
48. Singh, *Big Bang*, 298–99. Tegmark, *Our Mathematical Universe*, 104.

cause the mass in the Planck Era was nearly infinite in density, it contained all the energy needed for the inflationary epoch and the subsequent evolution of the universe.

Regarding the equivalence of mass and energy, we can consider three possibilities as to how this originated. The first, which we've considered before, posits that the Creator made it that way. The equivalence, in other words, is a manifestation of the Creator's will and acumen regarding the laws of physics. Second, we can suppose the equivalence is a consequence of the nature of matter itself. In this view, it was only matter that emanated from the Creator and the equivalence of mass and energy flowed automatically from that, requiring no intervention of will or intention on the Creator's part. Third, we can imagine that the equivalence is a manifestation of an aspect of the Creator's nature. It flowed automatically from His nature and became embedded in the physical laws that govern the universe.

I want to consider the third option in order to stick with the principles of interpretation that we have employed thus far. Accordingly, we would ask: What was it about the Creator's intrinsic nature that was manifested in the equivalence of mass and energy? By itself, "equivalence" speaks to a common substance or essence shared equally by two or more things. The shared essence is what makes them the same. They may not be identical in all respects, but they are identical when it comes to their essence. If we look at two ponderosa pines, for example, we will see that they are not identical. But they have the same essence. In philosophy, "essence" refers to the quality that makes something what it is. The two tress are both ponderosa pines; that's their shared essence.

The equivalence of mass and energy means they share the same essence, which could manifest the *oneness* of everything in God's nature; mass and energy are united there as one in essence. God is the common ground of their being.

Since everything in the universe exists either as mass or as energy, and because the *common essence* of mass and energy come from God, we can say that God is *in* everything, creating the essence of everything. In God, everything is one. (In chapter 6, we will encounter various descriptions of mystical experiences. A common aspect is the feeling that everything is one in God.)

We should also keep in mind what the equivalence of mass and energy accomplishes in creating our world. The mass of protons and neutrons carries energy, and it is this energy that binds their constituent quarks together.[49] Were this not the case, atoms would not exist. The universe would be a sea of unbound, aimless particles.

6. *Dark Matter and Dark Energy*. Cosmologists have found that galaxies are rotating with such speed that they should fly apart. There is a mysterious matter that keeps galaxies from spinning out of control; a substance that cannot be detected that adds the extra mass (and therefore gravity) needed to keep galaxies together.[50] This matter is not really dark; it is transparent to light. It neither emits nor absorbs light. Because it cannot be directly observed, it is *inferred* to exist because of the gravitational effect it has within galaxies and between clusters of galaxies.[51] But what is it? That remains one of the most dogged unanswered questions in cosmology today.

We also have the mystery of dark energy.[52] Something is causing the universe to expand at an ever-accelerating rate. General relativity tells us that the universe must have a certain amount of energy in order to be expanding the way it is. The total energy cosmologists can measure only accounts for about 30 percent of what's needed. The other 70 percent is dark. It must be there because of the way the universe is expanding. The missing or dark energy has other mysterious qualities. Somehow, it is distributed evenly throughout the universe and is not diluted as the universe expands.

Taking dark matter and dark energy together, they account for about 95 percent of the content of the universe. Cosmologists have many different ideas about the nature of dark matter and dark energy and have a number of investigations underway to unravel the underlying physics of such a large portion of the known universe.

Since the creation of the universe, there has been a tug-of-war between dark matter and dark energy, with neither getting the upper hand. It is most fortuitous for us that dark matter and dark energy are constituted and balanced the way they are.[53] If there was more dark matter, or if it was more dense, our universe would have collapsed upon itself. If there was less of it, or if it was less dense, then galaxies would have hurled their stars into deep space. If there was more dark energy, the runaway expansion of the universe would have prevented the necessary proximity of planets and stars for life to evolve. If there was less dark energy, gravity would get the upper hand and the universe would end in a big crunch. I will return to this topic later

---

49. Randall, *Knocking on Heaven's Door*, 84.
50. Singh, *Big Bang*, 478–80.
51. Randall, *Knocking on Heaven's Door*, 120.
52. Galfard, *Universe in Hand*, 292–302.
53. Tegmark, *Our Mathematical Universe*, 106–7, 140–41.

when I discuss the many ways our universe appears to be fine-tuned for us to be here.

Our question, of course, is what the fact of dark matter and dark energy might reveal about the Creator. We don't know what the dark matter consists of, and we don't know the source of the dark energy. We only know we are talking about matter and energy that are dark and invisible. Using the principle of emanation, we would posit that this matter and energy (whatever their makeup) emanated from God's nature. But what do they *manifest* about God? Because they emanated from God in a manner that was fine-tuned to the creation of galaxies and to a restrained (not run-away) expansion of the universe, we can infer that they reveal or manifest a purpose. We see that purpose only in the balance and fine-tuning of the matter and energy that emanated from the Creator. This purpose is inferential only . . . the purpose being the creation of a universe with galaxies and limited expansion, for this is what the balance of matter and energy brought about.

At the end of the day, of course, we are confronted with the limitations of our knowledge about the universe in which we find ourselves and about the nature of a Creator Deity. While we know a great deal about this universe, we are humbled by the existence of dark matter and dark energy, showing us how much we do not know. And regarding a Creator Deity, we are reminded again that anything we think we know about His nature is intrinsically *inferential*. When relying on the book of nature, as we are doing here, that is the best we can do.

7. *Causality and Randomness*. Before the advent of quantum mechanics, physicists believed the laws of cause and effect governed the entire universe and everything that happened therein. This was thought to be a deep truth about our world. Everything that existed and everything that happened was the *effect* of prior causes, and all these causes, taken together, *determined* the subsequent events. That is causal determinism in a nutshell. Einstein believed in it, and for reason, he did not believe in free will.[54] All of our thoughts and actions, he believed, are the determined result of prior causes.

This was the bedrock cornerstone of classical physics. Certainly in many situations it would not be possible to know all the casual factors, but still, the deterministic dogma held sway. Thus, cosmologist have been able, using known laws of physics and the principles of causality embedded in them, to trace the origin of the universe back to the big bang, wherein they ran up against the Planck-era wall I mentioned earlier (see p. 5).

---

54. Isaacson, *Einstein*, 391–93.

Causal determinism is obviously relevant to the method we have been using in this chapter. If this determinism is a fundamental aspect of reality that correctly describes the state of play in the universe, then we can speculate on what it might reveal about God's nature. Before we go down that path, however, we should look at the fundamental randomness of quantum mechanics, a randomness in the subatomic realm that throws a wrench in the works when it comes to thinking we live in a predictable world.

Physicists have done experiments relating to the location, momentum, and spin of subatomic entities such as electrons and photons, and whether these entities behave as particles or waves. The results of these experiments have been impossible to interpret using the causal determinism of classical physics. An alternative interpretation has arisen, an interpretation grounded in fundamental randomness. This interpretation and the resulting equations consistently work to explain experimental results that classical physics cannot explain.

The randomness interpretation holds that subatomic particles have features (such as location, momentum, and spin) that are not causally determined to be what they are. They do not obey deterministic laws. Random forces are in play in the quantum realm. Thus, particles there only obey equations that state the *probability* that they will be found, upon measurement, to have certain features.[55] Let's suppose you want to learn a particle's momentum and design an experiment. There is no way to predict what the result will be, because it is going to occur randomly, within certain probability limits. Before your experiment, an equation of quantum mechanics will give you the *probabilistic wave function* for the particle in question. The wave function gives the probability distribution for the particle—that is, the *likelihood* that it will have a certain momentum.[56] These experiments have proven "that a fundamental randomness is built into the laws of nature."[57]

You might want to argue that the result only *appears* to be random because all the causal factors are not known, and if they were known and could be factored in to the equations, then the result would be seen as casually determined. This interpretation, however, logically leads to conclusions that violate known laws of physics.[58] Most physicists, therefore, have come to embrace the randomness of quantum theory. Not all, however; some have held out that there must be a deeper order that explains the experimental results. Einstein, for example, could not accept the randomness of quantum

---

55. Tegmark, *Our Mathematical Universe*, 174–78.

56. Randall, *Knocking on Heaven's Door*, 74.

57. Tegmark, *Our Mathematical Universe*, 178.

58. Rovelli, *Seven Lessons*, 54–55.

mechanics. "I can't believe that God plays dice," he quipped. He believed the universe was ruled by deterministic laws, even if they were hidden from view in laboratory experiments.

The bottom line is that "quantum events are not determined absolutely by preceding causes."[59] This is because the quantum realm is a frenetic, swarming beehive of particles and forces dashing about in a chaotic and random manner.[60]

One of the mysteries of physics is that classical determinism works perfectly in the macroscopic world. Equations based on causal assumptions accurately describe what is going on in this world. But in the microscopic world such assumptions break down. How can nature be fundamentally random at the bottom-most level while producing results, higher up the chain, that are explained by classical physics? It seems the world of nature exists on two different and inconsistent levels. Perhaps the universe is intrinsically random but creates the illusion of causal determinism. Or perhaps the randomness of quantum mechanics is the illusion.

What might all of this say about the Creator? It would be easier to answer this question if either causal determinism or quantum randomness were a proven fact of how the world works at the most fundamental level. There is no proof one way or the other. There are only *interpretations* of what is going on, interpretations that appear better or worse at explaining experimental results.

I want to offer this possibility when it comes to God. I believe God found Himself having a certain nature, a nature that He did not create or even choose to have. He found principles of orderly causality within His nature, but also principles of chance occurrences and randomness. Presumably, He knew the world that would emanate from His nature would be mostly governed by causal laws, but He could also foresee random forces that would obey no laws. There are (apparently) no laws that govern randomness. Random events are lawless by definition; they happen spontaneously. Nonetheless, He allowed the universe to emanate from His nature because He believed the principles of orderly causality would win out . . . that on balance, the universe would unfold lawfully, keeping the threat of randomness in check. But win out for what purpose? That's what I want to explore next.

---

59. Davies, *Mind of God*, 61.
60. Rovelli, *Seven Lessons*, 65.

2

God's Purposes

I WANT TO THINK about God's purposes, about what they might be, and how we can best approach this essential question for the theology we are developing here. It's a question that concerns *our* purposes too. I say that because we are part of God's creation, so if we had some reasonable ideas about God's purposes, they would apply to us as well. To say this more succinctly: God's purposes would be our own.

Later in this chapter, I will be exploring three approaches we could take in order to derive some insight into God's purposes. Before jumping into that, however, there are some preliminary matters that need to be addressed.

First, supposing that God created the world to accomplish certain purposes involves the projection of human qualities onto God. Having purposes for our actions is something that humans do. Thus, assuming that God had purposes in mind, when bringing the universe into being, makes me guilty of anthropomorphizing, widely regarded as a sin in theology. It is the sin of attributing human motivations and characteristics to the divine Creator. There is no way of avoiding this sin, in my view, and I am not sure how grievous a sin it really is. In the previous chapter I argued that God is in us as the ground of our being. I maintained that the fundamental particles and forces in the atoms that comprise us emanated from God. Because these particles and forces eventually gave rise to human consciousness, it is not so far-fetched to suppose that the originator of these particles and forces was also a conscious being.

We are not only conscious; we are also rational. Our thought processes are logical ones. The logic that instills our minds must have a basis in the particles and forces that comprise our brains, particles and forces that ultimately came from God's nature. We have a basis, therefore, for supposing that God has a rational mind, and that our rational minds are a reflection of His. In other words, we inherited our rationality from God. Since we have a basis for thinking of God as a rational being, it is not much of a stretch to assume that God had a rational basis for the creation. There must have been a reason behind it, a reason *for* it.[1]

A second introductory point is this: the hypothesis of a purposeful God hinges on how we think of God's role in the creation. Here's what I mean. Some people believe God created the world to be the way it is, exercising His free choice. With regard to the fundamental building blocks and forces we are considering, these believers would say God freely *chose* these things to be what they are. The picture that comes to mind is that God, before the act of creation, had an array of physical laws to choose from, and that He chose the ones that gave rise to our universe. Or we could imagine that God was a spectacular genius and was able to create these laws from scratch.

The problem with this view, in my opinion, is that it raises the impossible question of why God did not create a more perfect world. Are we saying God freely chose to create a universe that would give rise to the kind of suffering we see all around us? Gottfried Leibniz, the eighteenth-century intellectual who made brilliant contributions to a variety of fields (including the philosophy of religion), famously argued that God created the best of all possible worlds. Thus, God should not be blamed for not making a better world.

As you know, I have a different view of how the creation came about. It goes like this. Before the creation, God was aware of His own nature (some aspects of which we speculated about in chapter 1). He found Himself having this nature, much in the same way that we find ourselves having a human nature. He did not create His own nature. Perhaps it existed infinitely, with no beginning. In any event, He knew what would emanate from His nature if He opted for a creation, as opposed to allowing nonbeing to prevail. He knew about the fundamental particles, forces, fields, and laws of physics that would emanate from His nature and the kind of universe that would unfold from there. He did not design these fundamental characteristics.

---

1. Davis, *Mind of God*, 161–222.

Again, they would flow seamlessly from His nature if He chose for that to happen. He obviously chose that, which is why we have the world we do. He chose for His nature to take flight in creating this world. That was God's creative *act*.

I believe it is reasonable to suppose that God, in letting the world take flight, had certain purposes in mind. Otherwise we'd be saying the creative act was mindless, having no intent. That seems absurd on the face of it. That God just let the creation happen for no good reason? Or that it happened accidently? Or that God was just curious about what would happen, or let the creation happen for the fun of it? Yes, it seems absurd to imagine that God was mindless or driven only by curiosity.

I am guilty again of anthropomorphizing. I can see that. I am now supposing that God was mindful, or thoughtful about what He was about to do, and that He had a certain motivation and intent. I see no way around this if we are to talk meaningfully about God's *purposes*.

The way I am imagining the creative act also implies a kind of weighing the pros and cons. I am saying that because, in my view, God was aware that His nature had certain elements of chaos, disorder, and randomness. He therefore knew that unlawful, random forces would be in play if He chose the creation. He could not predict what would happen. He'd be taking a risk, in other words. On the other hand, He was aware of elements of His nature that, in my view, would give rise to a universe filled with goodness, beauty, and love. He could also assess the likelihood of such a universe because of the lawful orderliness in His nature. This lawful orderliness would shore up His purpose and bolster the likelihood of its fulfillment over time. But this was not a sure thing because of those random elements. In other words, He had to weigh the pros and cons, as best He could envision them.

To summarize: I am suggesting that God had purposes, but that their fulfillment was not a sure thing. This view gets God off the hook, regarding the (evil) consequences of randomness. It also means we have a role to play in contributing to the fulfillment of God's purposes. There is a drama unfolding between the forces of goodness and the forces of evil. This is an age-old theological idea. We can be on the side of goodness and make a small but real difference (see ch. 3).

Just to clarify a certain point, I think that God could envision the fulfillment of His purposes only in the general characteristics of the universe as opposed to specific things that would happen, such as the evolution of mankind. In chapter 1, I surmised that His nature (before the creation) consisted of the initial conditions that He embodied. These conditions held the *potential* that was locked inside His nature. He must have known that this potential, once it was released, would become actualized in a certain kind of universe. This potential, in my view, did not predict specific events but only general characteristics.

Okay, I am done with my preliminary comments. Let's move on to the matter at hand.

How to Approach the Question of God's Purposes

First, I want to tackle the question of method. I don't believe this is as boring as it sounds. In thinking of God's purposes, what approach makes the most sense? In keeping with the method we employed in the last chapter, we would look at the universe itself (the book of nature) to see if it revealed anything about God's purposes.

We could look for God's purposes in three aspects of His creation:

1. The fundamental characteristics of the universe.
2. The evolution of the universe.
3. The fine-tuning of the universe to create life.

These three aspects are *of God*. The meaning of that phrase throughout this book is that something is *of God* if it (1) came from God (emerged from God as its source) and (2) reveals or manifests something about God. In this book's theology, the universe itself emerged out of God and reveals aspects of His purposes. The universe is *of God* and poses the following questions:

Do Its Fundamental Characteristics Reveal a Purpose?

Let me start this section with an analogy. Suppose we had the paintings of a certain artist, an artist who only painted scenes of nature and did so with exquisite detail and precision, so much so that her paintings looked like photographs. This precision would be the *fundamental characteristic* in all her paintings, regardless of the particular scene she painted. Having only her paintings to do go on, we could reasonably infer that her *purpose* was to render the reality of nature in a manner that was most true to that reality. Why did she only paint scenes of nature? Why did she do that with such precision? An understanding of her purposes would answer those questions.

Applying this approach to God's purposes, we could look at the many fundamental characteristics of the universe that emanated from His nature (heat, motion, force, matter, energy, fields, atoms, etc.) and base our inferences about His purposes from those characteristics. I will take one example just to illustrate how this approach could bear fruit.

One ubiquitous feature of the natural world concerns the laws of physics. Our world is built upon these laws in a (mostly) deterministic fashion. God's universe is a lawful one (mostly). These laws control the makeup of the universe and what happens therein. But do these laws tell us anything about God's purposes? I suppose they do, but only in the most rudimentary manner. They tell us that one purpose was to create a universe of law and order: the laws create the deterministic orderliness wherein everything that happens is the result of prior causes. But we want to ask: A lawful orderliness *for what purpose*, for what end, for what goal?

In other words, what do the laws that emanated from God *do*? On a fundamental level, they create whole things that consist of parts. Let me explain what I mean. Almost everything in the universe is comprised of parts that interact in ways that create whole entities. Take atoms, for example. They are whole things that have two parts (a nucleus and electrons). The nucleus is a whole consisting of two parts (protons and neutrons.) Protons and neutrons are not only *parts*, however. They are also whole things in their own right, but they consist of more fundamental parts (quarks). Atoms are also the parts that make up a molecule. This kind of part-whole relationship is a rudimentary characteristic of the created world. When we look at a whole entity, we don't see what it really is because we don't see the constituent parts hidden within it. We always must dig deeper to discover the truth about something.

Does this tell us anything about God's purposes? Well, the parts of whole entities, whatever they might be, always interact to create *harmony and balance* within the whole entities in question. We see this in the way the parts of an atom interact to create the whole atom. It appears that something is orchestrating the parts to interrelate in a harmonious and balanced manner. For example, protons in the nucleus repel each other with a certain force, but thankfully, this repulsion is balanced by a binding force that keeps the nucleus intact. Were these competing forces not perfectly balanced, there would be no atoms.[2]

Harmony and balance, however, do not always rule the day. The weak nuclear force, for example, causes large atoms such as uranium to break down and fall apart. While the smaller atoms that result from this process (called radioactive decay) are more stable, the process itself is essentially destructive.[3] The harmonious whole that had existed in the larger atom is

---

2. Greene, *Elegant Universe*, 13.
3. Singh, *Big Bang*, 158–59. Galfard, *Universe in Your Hand*, 17.

broken apart. This is part of a theme that we will encounter throughout this book—namely, there are destructive forces in the universe, such as the weak nuclear force and the endemic randomness that infects the universe, that run counter to God's creative purposes.

We also need to address a basic teleological question. What final purposes are served by harmony, balance, and the lawful orderliness of cause and effect? I do not believe they are ends in themselves. Atoms, for example, are not ends in themselves. They evolved in the early universe through a process of integration, wherein parts became wholes, but did not stop there. They gave rise to the universe we have. What kind of universe is it? What has happened here?

Does the Evolution of the Universe Reveal a Purpose?

Cosmologists and physicists have charted the evolution of the universe from the big bang to the formation of our solar system,[4] and some have taken up the story to chart the 4.5 billion years of our home planet.[5] Because this evolution has so many different facets and chapters, I want to focus only on two of the most fundamental aspects: the initial formation of atoms, and the role of stars in the creation and propagation of atoms throughout the universe.

There were no atoms in the moments following the big bang. The formation of atoms would require many steps, and they would all come later. First, quarks would have to bind in groups of three to create protons and neutrons. Then the protons and neutrons would have to bind to form nuclei. In the final step, positively-charged protons would need to capture negatively-charged electrons. In the first few seconds, it was much too hot and chaotic for any of that to happen. About one minute after the big bang, however, hydrogen protons and neutrons came into existence and were then fused to create (mostly) hydrogen and helium nuclei. These were the first nuclei, and the process of their formation is called primordial nucleosynthesis. The universe continued to expand and cool, and after about three hundred thousand years, the "wildly streaming electrons," which had been too chaotic to reign in, slowed down enough to be captured by the hydrogen and helium nuclei, thus creating the first electrically-neutral atoms (neutral because the opposite charges of the protons and electrons were balanced or neutralized).

The nascent universe was essentially a cosmic fusion reactor converting hydrogen, which was a billion degrees hot, into helium. This process

---

4. Greene, *Elegant Universe*, 345–46. Tegmark, *Our Mathematical Universe*, 34–67.
5. Hazen, *Story of Earth*.

stopped when the universe cooled, but it was taken up again within the core of stars, where the gravitational energy and pressure created sufficient heat to create atoms by nuclear fusion. Thus, stars have been called "huge thermonuclear-fusion power plants."[6] Early on, stars mostly created helium, with a smattering of deuterium and lithium. But in their later stages, they turned helium into carbon, oxygen, and most of the other atoms we are made of. Because of the processes within the heart of stars, light and particles are blown outward and contribute to the formation of other stars. But stars also explode, and their atoms are blown far and wide and are eventually recycled into gas clouds, new stars, planets, and creatures such as us. Thanks to the atom-creating activity within stars and thanks also to the explosion of stars, the universe became replete with all the elements that now exist. Everything owes their existence, as far as their atomic makeup goes, to the residue of stars. "We are all made of star stuff."[7]

I have reviewed this evolution of the universe to underscore a key point related to God's purposes: atoms and stars are *of God* because their foundational, constituent components emanated from God's nature. Atoms and stars were not directly made by God but their constituent components were.

The evolution of atoms and stars indicates that we all have a common source and share the same *fundamental* makeup. At bottom, we are all made of the constituent particles and forces within atoms. And because these came from God, we are all children of God in that sense. This is more basic than sharing the same DNA with an identical twin. It is a common ground of being that we share. And we share this, not just with each other, but with all creatures and with all of reality. We all belong to each other, and we belong to our world, and our world and its creatures belong to us.

Could God foresee that atoms and stars would evolve in the way they did, creating an essential commonality among all things composed of atoms? Yes, I believe He could foresee that, and it points to a purpose behind the creation. But there must be more to it, in my mind. What is this essential commonality *for*? What good is it; what purposes does it serve? I like to think it would cause us to love each other more, and to love our planet more. Leaving us aside, I like to think that God wants all beings everywhere to be more bound up with each other in facing the conditions of our shared existence.

---

6. Galford, *Universe in Hand*, 17.
7. Tegmark, *Our Mathematical Universe*, 64.

Does the Fine-Tuning of the Universe Reveal a Purpose?

Many cosmologists and physicists have discussed the fine-tuning of the universe to give rise to atoms, stars, planets, and life. This fine-tuning means that if a given parameter (the strength of a force, the amount of dark matter, for example) were ever so slightly different, then we would not be here to talk about it. A leading astronomer at Cambridge University has devoted an entire book to this topic,[8] although he focused only on six parameters. There are apparently many more examples of fine-tuning than that.[9] I will discuss just two examples of this fine-tuning, both of which are quite startling.

The first example refers back to the discussion of dark matter and dark energy (ch. 1, pp. 31–2). These need to be perfectly balanced or the universe would be in big trouble. If there was more dark matter, or if its density was greater, its gravity would have pulled the universe back into what is called the big crunch. On the other hand, if there was more dark energy, or if it was more energetic, it would have caused the universe to fly apart, long before galaxies could form. These two forces—the pulling-together force of dark matter and the pushing-apart force of dark energy—must be perfectly balanced for our universe to be the way it is.

How "perfectly balanced" am I talking about? Well, the current amount of dark energy that's been measured is about 10^{-27} kilograms per cubic meter.[10] This is close to zero dark energy when compared to the maximum amount allowable in quantum physics, which is 10^{97} kilograms per cubic meter. Now, let's suppose you have a knob that can adjust the amount of dark energy in the universe. If you rotate the knob a full turn, you'd cover 360 degrees, but there are many more settings (or angle points) around the knob than 360. In fact, there are nearly an infinite number of possible settings, so the knob can be turned ever so slightly in either direction. Now, your job is to point the knob to the correct setting, so the amount of dark energy is not too great or too small. "To accomplish this feat, you'd have to get the angle right by over 120 decimal places. Although this sounds like an impossible fine-tuning task, some mechanism appears to have done precisely this for our Universe."[11]

We have already discussed the strong nuclear force that binds protons and neutrons in the nucleus of atoms (ch. 1, pp. 24–5). Let's now consider the strength of that force. It turns out that it had to be *just so* . . . that is,

---

8. Rees, *Just Six Numbers*.
9. Tegmark, *Our Mathematical Universe*, 137.
10. Tegmark, *Our Mathematical Universe*, 141.
11. Tegmark, *Our Mathematical Universe*, 141.

if it were slightly stronger or slightly weaker, the consequences would be catastrophic for the universe and for us.

Let's take the slightly weaker scenario, weaker by a mere one-thousandth of its actual strength. Had this been the case, then the fusion of hydrogen into deuterium, helium, and all the other heavier elements would not have occurred. The entire universe would consist only of bland hydrogen and thus no chance for life.[12] What about the slightly stronger scenario? Let's suppose the force was just one-thousandth stronger than its actual value? Then hydrogen would have transformed itself into other elements right after the big bang, leaving no hydrogen left over to fuel the stars. In other words, the strength of this force needed to be spot-on; if it didn't have the value it actually has, we would not be here to be in awe of this most fortuitous circumstance.[13]

What are we to make of this fine-tuning? It *appears* that the universe was designed to evolve in just the way it did, giving rise to atoms, stars, and life. The evolution of human life too—made possible by certain atoms, molecules, and environmental circumstances—was contingent on this fine-tuning. It has been argued that this fine-tuning reveals the will and purpose of the Creator, a being who designed the universe for our ultimate benefit.[14]

As you know already, the God of this book's theology did not "design" the universe to be the way it is or to achieve any particular purpose. I believe the fundamental building blocks and forces in nature flowed or emanated from God's nature, which He did not design or create. But God must have known, in my view, that His nature would give rise to the laws of physics and initiate a chain of causality driven by those laws. These laws were not literally God; rather, they were *of* God: they came from God and manifested aspects of His nature. The chain of causality resulting from these laws would lead to a universe with certain characteristics that would enable life to flourish. These characteristics are precisely the fine-tuning we've discussed. God allowed the creation to take off in the direction it did, knowing this would result in a universe with characteristics conducive to life. So, in that sense we owe this fine-tuning to God's nature and to what God intended to happen.

Quantum Field Theory (ch. 1, pp. 25–8) can help to support this point of view. The theory posits that various fields permeate all of space and cause certain things to happen. The strong force field, for example, binds protons and neutrons together wherever in the universe they may happen to be. This field could be seen as one manifestation of God's nature and indicative of

---

12. Singh, *Big Bang*, 486.
13. See also Rees, *Just Six Numbers*, 54–57.
14. Polkinghorne, *Quarks, Chaos, and Christianity*.

God's intentionality. It exerted a foundational and formative influence on the evolution of the universe. It can help explain why the universe evolved with the fine-turning in question.

These theological speculations about the fine-tuning are not embraced by most physicists. The more common explanation is simply logical. It goes like this: Of course the universe had to be the way it is, because if it was not this way, we would not be here to wonder about it. The fact that we are here means that it *had* to be "fine-tuned" for the eventual evolution of human life. According to this view, there is no mystery or wonderment about it.

There is also the view that the fine-tuning is just a colossal fluke . . . a fortuitous coincidence that enabled us to evolve. We are just extraordinarily lucky for the universe to be fine-tuned the way it is. Proponents of this view are not saying the fine-tuning happened *by accident*. They are saying the *chain of causality* unleashed in the big bang was lawful (not accidental) and resulted in a universe with the *precise* parameters necessary for the evolution of life and, what's more, that the odds against this happening by coincidence alone are staggering. And yet it *was* by coincidence alone that they happened. This is what is meant by a colossal fluke.

Then there is the theory that our universe is just one of an infinite number of universes that currently exist or that have existed in the past. For example, the big bang may eventually result in the big crunch, causing another big bang and then another big crunch, a process of birth, death, and rebirth that could go on eternally. Or the big bang that we know about could, based on the laws of physics, have created an infinite number of universes simultaneously. If we are talking about an infinite number of universes, then sooner or later there would be one that appeared fine-tuned for us.[15]

Some physicists have been rightly humble in admitting that no one really knows why the universe is fine-tuned the way it is. The universe is the way it is because the matter and force particles have the properties they do . . . but "no one has any explanation of why."[16]

On to chapter 3 . . .

---

15. For a fascinating discussion of these possibilities, see Tegmark, *Our Mathematical Universe*, 119–53.

16. Greene, *Elegant Universe*, 12.

3

God's Purposes in Relation to Goodness, Beauty, and Love

IN THE LAST TWO chapters I turned to the book of nature and certain characteristics of the universe to see what they might reveal about God's nature and purposes. There was a clear logic to this approach, the same logic that informed the thinking of Newton and Einstein, to name the two giants of this approach. The logic was simply this: If we start by assuming the existence of a Creator Deity, then the best way of exploring His nature and purposes is to look directly at what He created.

I am taking a different approach in this chapter. I start with three working hypotheses about God's purposes that are borrowed from a longstanding tradition in theology and religious philosophy—namely, that God created the universe to propagate His goodness, beauty, and love. Then I look back to the book of nature and the universe itself (in the ways we have explored them) to see if they support these hypotheses. That is, do we actually find manifestations of goodness, beauty, and love in the created world?

The problem with this approach is that we have to start—we are doomed to start—with *human* definitions of goodness, beauty, and love. It would be most prideful and anthropomorphically audacious to suppose that these human concepts are applicable to God's purposes. And that's not the only problem. If we are to look for manifestations of goodness, beauty, and love in the created world, we need to know what we are looking *for*. That is, what is the true essence of these three qualities? What does it mean for something to be "good"? What makes something beautiful? What *is* love, really? We need to have a handle on these matters.

I will admit a personal bias here, a bias that you might share: It is an *appealing* notion to suppose that God created the universe to propagate goodness, beauty, and love. As I mentioned above, this is also a bias, and an assumption, in much of theology and in theistic and deistic philosophy. To judge the universe (and by implication, the Creator) as being good, beautiful, or loving is a value judgment on our part. But it seems reasonable to search for value in God's creation because God did not create a valueless universe. If God did not instill some value in the creation then it would be pointless and purposeless.

If you are with me at this point, then we should proceed as follows. First, we should try to conceptualize, as best we can, the objective essence of goodness, beauty, and love. Next, we would aim to discern whether, and how, these three qualities are manifested in God's creation. Finally, we would infer that these qualities must be part of God's purpose, on the basis that they would not be in God's creation if they were not meant to be there.

Our wanting to know the *essence* of goodness, beauty, and love puts us into the realm of metaphysics. The essence of something is an abstract quality that makes something what it is. It is metaphysical because it is abstract and presumably immaterial. You can do a little metaphysics right now by thinking of all the people you know who are good and then asking yourself: What is that ingredient they all share in common that makes them good? If you could nail that down you would know the essence of the goodness manifested in the people you know.

Knowing the *objective* nature of a value is a real can of worms. By "objective," I mean the nature of a value as it really exists, independent of any human conceptualization of it. It goes without saying, therefore, that we cannot know the objective essence of goodness, beauty, and love because our thinking is ultimately subjective. We are stuck with human minds. However, if we can agree that they *have* an objective essence, and that this could tell us something about God's purposes, then it seems worthwhile to try our best to get at that essence.

I wonder how much you know about Plato or if you have even heard of Alfred North Whitehead. I have the utmost admiration for these two philosophers because they did their very best to discern the objective truth regarding goodness and beauty. They started with the conviction that goodness and beauty are objectively *out there* in the universe, and in our natural world—and that these objective realities speak to God's purposes—and they have developed metaphysical systems to help define what goodness and beauty essentially are. It seems a worthwhile effort: otherwise we just have to throw up our hands in despair of ever grasping God's purposes.

I will turn to Plato first, to his metaphysics and how he conceived of the objective *essence* of goodness and beauty. Next I will turn to the metaphysics of Alfred North Whitehead for his understanding of objective beauty. Then I want to look at the standards for beauty in modern physics (theoretical physicists, for example, are fond of saying they see beauty in the basic laws of physics). Finally, I will look at what philosophy tells us about the true nature of love.

Goodness and Beauty in Plato's Metaphysics[1]

Plato had a burning desire to establish the objective reality of "the Good." In *The Republic*, he wanted to assert that statesmen should be educated to know the Good ... the Good with a capital G, not just someone's subjective opinion about what was good and what was not. To make that assertion, Plato himself needed a theory about the *essence* of the Good.

His theory started with the creation of the world, which he attributed to the Demiurge, a godlike figure best thought of as a kind of Divine Craftsman. To create the world, the Craftsman drew upon the eternal model of the Good,[2] a model that held the pure essence of goodness itself. Plato called this the Form of the Good. (When Plato uses the term "Form," it might be helpful to translate that in your mind to "essence.") Because the Craftsman wanted to create a world full of goodness, He drew upon the Form of the Good, which imparted goodness to all good things.

The Craftsman also wanted to create a world full of beauty, and to do that, He drew upon the Form of Beauty Itself, which was also part of the eternal model for an ideal universe. Beauty Itself imparts beauty to all beautiful things and receives its own goodness from the Form of the Good.

I want to emphasize that, for Plato, goodness and beauty were metaphysically real, eternal entities that existed independent of our awareness of them. They had objective reality, even though they were nonmaterial or spiritual in nature. Even if humans never existed, there would still be goodness and beauty in the universe. Moreover, the Forms for goodness

---

1. My source for this section comes primarily from Silverman, "Plato's Middle Period Metaphysics and Epistemology."
2. Archer-Hind, *The Timaeus of Plato*, 28a6.

and beauty also have a theological meaning for Plato because they inspired the Divine Craftsman in putting goodness and beauty in the created world.

We never encounter the pure essence of things; we only encounter the earthly manifestations of essences in the real objects they inform. These are called form-copies, not the Form itself.[3] Thus, we never encounter the Form of the Good and Plato never really defines what the Good is, just that it is a Form that gives good things their *essential* goodness.

We want to ask of Plato's philosophy: What does it mean for something or someone to be good? But the answer is mostly abstract and circular. Something is good if it has the essence of goodness, derived from the Form of the Good.

There are some clues, however, to what Plato means by the Good. He said the Good gives Truth to things known and the power to know in the knower.[4] In other words, the truth of something comes from the Good, so that whatever is true is also good. Moreover, to *know* what is true, well, that also is good. He also said the rational, mathematical order in the world was an expression of the Good. Other Forms are good in so far as they possess this same intelligible order.

So far we are only getting hints from Plato about the meaning of goodness. The truth is good, anything true is also good, and to know the truth is good. There is one more thing: A certain power is needed to know the truth, and this also comes from the Good.

There are further clues in Plato's philosophy of Being.[5] Be forewarned that things get a little abstract here, but I will do my best to clarify Plato's meaning. We can start with the meaning of "Being." Things don't just exist; they are *being* what they are. Look outside at a tree, any tree actually. It is *being* a tree. It has the essence of treeness, but it also has "beingness," which is a kind of power to be what it is, a tree. The beingness of things is derived from Being Itself, one of those pesky Forms in the model for an ideal universe, the model the Demiurge drew upon. Being Itself empowers things *to be*, to be something instead of nothing, while their essence defines what they are. The beingness of things is Good. That is the main point: it is good for things to be, to participate in Being Itself, which is Good.

These are startling metaphysical ideas. Plato is saying that for us *to be* who and what we are takes a certain *power* that is derived from Being Itself. We are empowered beings, and the power that enables us to be is good. In chapter 6 we will look at Paul Tillich's conception of God as the Ground of

---

3. Bostock, *Plato's Phaedo*, 102.
4. Adams, *Republic of Plato*, book V.
5. Archer-Hind, *Timaeus*, 27d5–28a1.

Being. Tillich was very influenced by Plato. Thus, the Ground of Being, in Tillich's theology, is also the Power of Being and Being Itself.

There is something else in Plato's creation story that is relevant to our question about goodness. The Forms that the Divine Craftsman drew upon were only abstract essences that had the potential to become something real. The Craftsman made them real in the created world via their participation in Being Itself, which is good. The point for our purposes is that it is good for things to be real, not just having the potential to be real. Potential itself that does not become anything real is not good.

Plato never referred to the creation story in the book of Genesis where God took stock of His creation and said that it was good. We can imagine the Divine Craftsman doing the same thing—seeing the goodness in the natural world because of the causal power of the Form of the Good to make it so.[6] His philosophy of Being is consistent with this idea. The creation is good because everything is sustained by the power of Being, which is Good.

In other words, if the universe is truly good, and indeed was made to be good by Plato's creator, then we have a basis for thinking that such goodness shows God's purpose.

If we summarize all this, in trying to parse out what Plato means by the Good, we would conclude:

- The truth is good.
- The power to know the truth is good.
- Rational, mathematical order is good.
- Realness is good, as compared to potential only.
- It is good for things to be, to participate in Being.
- The Good has causal power to create goodness in the world.

In other words, it is good when Being emanates into our world and manifests itself as a real thing (a particular form). When this happens, potential becomes real, and this is good.

These points put some flesh on the abstract bone called the Form of the Good. As I said, the Good exists abstractly, metaphysically, and eternally before any concrete manifestation of goodness occurs. The job of the Demiurge was to make the Good real in the world. *This was the purpose of creation.*

Plato's creator had a purpose, which was goodness, and our human purpose is the same. Our role is to emulate the Good and to make it real in

---

6. This causal power of The Good is put forth most distinctly in the *Phaedo*, 99c6. Cf. Bostock citation above.

the world.[7] What this means, I think, is that we should know and speak the truth, and that we should take hold of our inner potential and make it real.

Plato can also help us with the concept of intrinsic beauty, the way in which the created world is beautiful, and how beauty can also be understood as part of God's purpose.

We can start with Beauty Itself, which is the essence of beauty, and things are beautiful by virtue of partaking in this essence.[8] Just as Plato found the created world as being good, he also found it beautiful and reasoned back to the origin of this beauty in the Form of Beauty Itself, which his Craftsman drew upon in creating the world. Plato is struck not just by beauty, but by the fact that the universe is *supremely beautiful*, and this he attributed to the intelligence and goodness of the Divine Craftsman and to the supreme beauty of Beauty Itself. Thus, the beauty in the world is purposeful and divine in origin.

In *The Symposium*, Plato must have been speaking from his own experience when he says to Socrates that if a person encounters a number of beautiful things in the world, and can then discern the essence which makes them all beautiful, that person would have attained a vision of the very soul of beauty, which makes life worth living.[9]

In the *Phaedrus*, Plato said that our souls had a vision of Beauty Itself before falling into bodily existence. Then, when we encounter beauty in the world, our souls are drawn back to thoughts of absolute beauty, which informs and enhances our appreciation of beauty.[10] It's a lovely idea, in my opinion.

We could ask of Plato's philosophy the same type of question we posed regarding goodness: What does it mean for something or someone to be beautiful? The *abstract* answer is found in his metaphysics: It means that the thing or person in question is informed with the essence of beauty, derived from Beauty Itself. If we then ask: What does it mean to partake in Beauty Itself? The answer: It means to be beautiful. That merry-go-round doesn't help us much.

The close relationship between the Form of the Good and Beauty Itself sheds some light on what Plato means by beauty.[11] He says the Good is the source of Beauty, so that when something is beautiful it reflects the goodness of its source. Beauty Itself, however, not only manifests the Good (which is

---

7. Adams, *Republic*, book V.
8. See Plato, *Symposium*, 206e–207a. See also Bostock, *Phaedo*, 100c3–7.
9. Plato, *Symposium*, 210a–211d.
10. See Plato, *Phaedrus*, 247c–d.
11. Plato, *Symposium*, 201c, 205e.

its source), it also subsumes and unifies all the different manifestations of beautiful things. The various beautiful things in the world are form copies of Beauty, all of which find their unification in Beauty Itself.[12] Beauty Itself, in other words, has it all!

Plato's metaphysics allows us draw on our human experience of beauty in order to grasp the essence of Beauty Itself. This is because our subjective experience of beauty carries a recollection of our soul's vision of the essence of Beauty before our bodily existence.[13] Thus, this essence could not be dissimilar to what we mean, in human terms, when we say something or someone is beautiful.

In *The Symposium*, Plato refers to the essence of beauty as spiritual loveliness and that beauty can also exist in laws and institutions. Later in this chapter, we will visit the search for beauty in the laws of quantum mechanics to illustrate how laws can be beautiful in a Platonic sense.

To summarize, let's return to our question of what Beauty really is. Plato only tells us that:

- Beauty is good, by definition.
- Everything that is beautiful is made so by partaking in Beauty Itself.
- There is but one essence to Beauty, which unifies all beautiful things.
- Beauty is spiritually lovely.
- Grasping the essence or soul of Beauty makes life worth living.

I can't help but admire what Plato is trying grasp—namely, the real essence or soul of Beauty. It's out there, in that metaphysical realm, just being what it is, independent of our apprehension of it. But insofar as we appreciate its essence, a divine purpose of the universe is revealed to us.

As I said in the beginning of this chapter, our approach is to arm ourselves with a conception of what goodness and beauty essentially are, and then see if this goodness and beauty are actually manifested in the created world. Such a manifestation would bolster the notion that the promulgation of goodness and beauty speak to God's purposes in the creation.

Certainly the created world is bursting with manifestations of goodness and beauty, as we conceptualize them. But remember, in Plato's philosophy *our* discernment of goodness and beauty is relevant to what goodness

---

12. Plato, *Symposium*, 210a–11d. This idealistic conception of beauty as perfect unity is distinct from the classical conception, wherein beauty "consists of an arrangement of integral parts in a coherent whole, according to proportion, harmony, symmetry and similar notions." Sartwell, "Beauty," 7–9.

13. See Plato, *Phaedrus*, 247c–d.

and beauty really *are*, because our souls encountered their essence before our earthly existence.

We also find that the created world *is real* and therefore good . . . and beautiful too by extension, because the Good is the source of Beauty. Every real thing in the creation is also *being* what it is. Being Itself (which embodies the Form of the Good) is manifested in the beingness of all things, in their power to be what they are. In chapter 1, when discussing the initial conditions that resulted in the big bang, I mentioned how they embodied the *potential* for the universe to unfold as it did. This pure potential, in Plato's view, would not itself be Good; the goodness would be found in the creation, wherein the potential became real. In the act of creation, it was Being Itself that burst forth and gave beingness and realness to all things.

I believe what Plato is getting at is this: The created world is intrinsically good and beautiful because it is real and because Being Itself is manifested in it.

Let's see if Alfred North Whitehead can help us be more specific about the nature of beauty.

Beauty in the Metaphysics of Alfred North Whitehead

Alfred North Whitehead (1861–1947) was an English mathematician and philosopher, best known as the founding father of process philosophy. He was a distinguished Harvard Professor from 1924–1937.

Whitehead views reality as a constant process of change, a process wherein everything is "in flow," as Whitehead put it. I offer the brief summary below in hopes of giving a sense of the flow in his metaphysical system:

> Anything that exist is not only a real thing (an "actual entity," in Whitehead's terms); it is also bursting with potential to be part of something new *and* is already in the process of becoming something new. This new actual entity will embody at least some of the potential that created it and, at the same time, it becomes a potentiality for something new. Nothing is standing still, and there are no *fixed* essences. Instead, everything in Whitehead's world is in a *dynamic* process wherein potentialities become actual, and these actual entities (by virtue of their relationship with other entities) are part of the process that creates ever-new possibilities for the future.

Whitehead is looking at the world and attempting to describe what is *really* going on. Direct observation can only go so far. His method, which he calls "imaginative generalization," seeks to penetrate the hidden dynamics

GOD'S PURPOSES IN RELATION TO GOODNESS, BEAUTY, AND LOVE   53

at work. He seldom offers concrete examples, but those that best illuminate his thought involve our personal experience. When you woke up this morning, there were countless possibilities for what to do or think, and you had to do or think something. You were caught in a creative process. Whatever you did or thought involved the actualization of some of the possibilities awaiting you, whereby you became a new actual entity (not a new person, but something new now existed in you and for you) and this newness was woven into the web of possibilities for what you would do and think next.

For Whitehead, reality is always flowing toward novel actualizations, but not in a blind or value-free way. There is value in all actuality because the process of actualization is one wherein potentialities become real.[14] We see in this an echo of Plato's idea that having potential is not as good as being real. For Whitehead, some of the things that become real are judged to be better than others, and this is where Beauty enters in.

Because of God's role in the creative advance (see below), the process always opts for *the fullest possible* realization or actualization of the potentialities available at the time. Any actuality that represents a less than optimum realization of the potential available to it is simply less than what it might have been. When this happens, the creative potentiality in the process is thwarted; God's purposes are thwarted, which is a manifestation of evil.[15] It would be no better to have *all* the available possibilities realized; this would result in chaos, since some possibilities are always incompatible. Nor would it be good to simply realize all the *compatible* possibilities, as that would result in a dull and boring outcome ("a tameness of outworn perfection," as Whitehead put it), an outcome that would offer little freshness and novelty for the future.

Hang on for a second, as we are getting to the concept of Beauty and God's purpose. Given the dilemma posed in the preceding paragraph, Whitehead proposes a blending of maximum *harmony* with maximum *intensity*, which is his definition of Beauty.[16]

Let's take harmony first. The process wherein new actualities are created always entails a coming together of relevant possibilities, but some of these possibilities are always incompatible. These incompatibilities can thwart the creative process because of the conflict and inhibition between them. Harmony is the *absence* of this kind of destructiveness.[17] It involves

---

14. Whitehead, *Religion in the Making*, 97.
15. Whitehead, *Religion*, 94.
16. Whitehead, *Adventure of Ideas*, 265.
17. Whitehead, *Adventure*, 276–78.

the *harmonious blending* of the relevant possibilities. That's the first step toward Beauty.

When there is too much harmony, however, then intensity suffers, and intensity is equally important in the creation of Beauty. Intensity refers to the *dynamic contrasts* that can result when the relevant possibilities come together in a new entity or experience.[18] It occurs when the contrasts between incompatible possibilities are interwoven and patterned in a way that provides for mutual support, enhancement, and creativity. With intensity, things become more definite, vivid, and bursting with novel possibilities for the future.

Without intensity, harmony would degenerate into timid mediocrity. And without harmony, intensity would become chaotic and destructive. Thus, Whitehead's concept of Beauty integrates both principles. It's a concept that borrows from principles of composition in music and painting:

> We can say that the colors harmonize, the masses balance, the total effect is forceful owing to strong contrasts of color or shape, and that force centers on a few points of emphasis which are enhanced by the richness of duly subordinated detail. In such principles of art Whitehead finds general standards of valuation.[19]

The fullest realization and manifestation of value is in Beauty. Any actuality in Whitehead's system has some value because it represents the realization of at least some possibility or potential. But with harmony, maximum possibilities are conjoined without inhibition or destruction. And with intensity, dynamic and creative contrasts are formed, opening maximum possibilities for future fulfillment. It is only by being beautiful that an actuality fulfills the potential given to it by the creative process.[20]

In Whitehead's metaphysics, God lures and persuades the world in the direction of Beauty. This is God's purpose in the creative advance.[21] As one scholar wrote:

> God seeks in his experience of the world the maximum attainment of intensity compatible with harmony under the circumstances of the actual situation. God provides to each occasion that initial aim which, if actualized, would contribute maximally to this harmonious intensity (Beauty). This is the aim God wills

---

18. Whitehead, *Adventure*, 252.
19. Morgan, "Whitehead's Theory of Value," 313.
20. Whitehead, *Religion*, 100.
21. Whitehead, *Process and Reality*, 160.

GOD'S PURPOSES IN RELATION TO GOODNESS, BEAUTY, AND LOVE 55

as good for each creature in his role as the dynamic source of value.[22]

As Whitehead himself describes God's purpose in the world: "He is the poet of the world, with tender patience leading it by his vision of truth, beauty, and goodness."[23]

It would be good to appreciate, I think, what Whitehead is attempting to do in his theory about Beauty. He wants to capture what Beauty *is* at its most fundamental level. This is similar to the quest of quantum physics to uncover the fundamental building blocks and forces in matter itself. For Whitehead, wherever Beauty exists, whether it's a galaxy or an atom, it is born from an optimum balance and integration of harmony and intensity. There is nothing more fundamental or constituent of Beauty; nothing at a deeper level that makes something beautiful.

There is something else that would be good to appreciate, I believe. In chapter 2, I noted that one ubiquitous feature of the natural world concerns the laws of physics, and that one of the fundamental things these laws do is to create whole things consisting of parts. Almost everything in the universe, I said, is comprised of parts that interact in ways that create whole entities. Whitehead's metaphysics help us appreciate how this part-whole interaction can create Beauty, and how this is an aspect of God's purpose. It appears that something is orchestrating the parts to interrelate in a harmonious and balanced manner. In Whitehead's view, this is how God persuades and lures the universe in the direction of Beauty.

We see in the world of particle physics that the world is sometimes beautiful, and sometimes not. In physics, there must be a balance of competing forces for our world to be relatively stable. Oftentimes this balance is present, which is also necessary for Beauty. In the cosmos at large, however, the force of gravity is not balanced with the force of dark energy; consequently, the universe is expanding at an ever-increasing rate. The intensity of the dark energy is overwhelming the pull of gravity, compromising the beauty of the whole.

A good example of beauty in our solar system is seen in the stable orbits of planets around the sun and the orbit of the moon around earth. The intense energy behind the motion of planets would cause them to fly off into space if this energy was not balanced by the gravity of the sun.

Einstein's theory of gravity is that anything with mass curves the space around it and that objects within that space move in accordance with this curvature. The planets in our solar system are caught in the curvature

---

22. Ford, "Divine Persuasion," 242–43.
23. Whitehead, *Process*, 526.

created by the sun, and a beautiful Whiteheadian balance of harmony and intensity is achieved. With black holes, however, the curvature is so extreme that nothing can orbit within it; instead, anything caught in this curvature will cascade toward the black hole and be lost forever. In other words, black holes create a gravity that is too intense.

I think it is fair to say that in nature we see the pull toward harmony and the force of intensity and that, yes, sometimes they appear in proper balance and result in beauty, in Whitehead's scheme. And, he believes, this is God's doing and God's purpose.

The Concept of Beauty in Modern Physics

Certainly since the days of Isaac Newton, physicists have been searching for beauty in the laws of nature. In recent times, a consensus has emerged that beauty is a reliable guide to truth.[24] In theoretical physics, for example, some equations relating to particle interactions are seen as more beautiful than others, and the bias now is that the more beautiful equations are probably more correct or true. But what do physicists mean by beauty?

This is an important question for us because it pertains to God's purpose when it comes to beauty. In the tradition of Plato and Whitehead, many scientists today assume that certain things are *objectively* beautiful. A mathematical theorem, for example, can be thought to have *intrinsic* beauty. Einstein, for one, believed that the beauty in nature's laws reflected God's mind and purpose. "I want to know how God created this world," Einstein said, "I want to know his thoughts."[25]

The meaning of beauty in modern physics is somewhat general and vague, although certain concepts are commonly employed to convey what is meant by the "beauty" of nature's laws, and these concepts are worth reviewing.

Einstein saw beauty in the rationality, elegance, and simplicity of the laws governing the universe.[26] He saw the universe as beautifully designed, and attributed this to the mind of God. He believed God used the simplest conceivable mathematical laws in creating our world. Interestingly, he reasoned that if God could have conceived of more simple and elegant laws, he would have done so.

---

24. Davies, *Mind of God*, 175–77.

25. Salaman, *Talk with Einstein* (Third Program), 370–71. See also Jammer, *Einstein and Religion*, 123.

26. Isaacson, *Einstein*, 384–93.

GOD'S PURPOSES IN RELATION TO GOODNESS, BEAUTY, AND LOVE 57

To Einstein, the laws employed by God exhibited an awe-inspiring rationality grounded in a transcendent order.[27] Einstein was a Platonist in that sense. This rationality was seen in how these laws made such simple sense and how they were related to each other and fit together with an astounding, intricate arrangement (another criterion of beauty). If an equation failed to live up to these standards of beauty, he considered it ugly and would not entertain it.[28] It could not be true if it was not beautiful.

The theoretical physicists Brian Greene, in *The Elegant Universe*,[29] and Anthony Zee, in *Fearful Symmetry: The Search for Beauty in Modern Physics*,[30] emphasize symmetry as a main criterion for beauty. A sphere is the simplest example of what physicists mean by symmetry. If you were to cut a sphere exactly in half, the two halves would be equal. A sphere also has what is called rotational symmetry. If you were to hold a ball in your hands and rotate it around or look at it from different angles, it would still look the same.

Physicists have discovered that physical reality has many symmetries built into it,[31] and for many, this reveals the beauty of creation. For example, particles that have the same charge interact with each other in exactly the same way that particles with the opposite charges interact.[32] These interactions are symmetrical, in other words.

Einstein's special relativity illustrates a symmetry in the speed of light—namely, that it's the same for anyone measuring it, from whatever perspective, so long as they are neither accelerating or decelerating. For example, suppose you have a rifle that can shoot a beam of light, the speed of which is defined by the laws of physics. On dry land, where you are neither accelerating or decelerating, you shoot the rifle and measure the speed of the light beam. Then you board a cruise ship and wait until it reaches 25 mph as a constant speed. You go to the back of the ship and shoot your rifle toward the front. The speed of the light beam will still be the same; it will not be the speed of light plus 25 mph. The speed of light is constant for everyone, no matter how fast they are moving, so long as their speed is uniform. This is called Lorentz symmetry and is built into the way light travels.[33]

---

27. Isaacson, *Einstein*, 385.
28. Davies, *Mind of God*, 175–76.
29. Greene, *Elegant Universe*, 124–26, 168–70.
30. Zee, *Fearful Symmetry*, ch. 1.
31. Tegmark, *Our Mathematical Universe*, 266–69.
32. Greene, *Elegant Universe*, 125.
33. Tegmark, *Our Mathematical Universe*, 338–39.

The laws of physics are also thought to have rotational symmetry in the sense that they work the same regardless of the orientation of an observer; for example, there is no special direction in our universe that can be considered "up."[34]

The physicist Paul Davies, in his book *The Mind of God*, tells the story of Paul Dirac, a theoretical physicist whose sense of beauty led him to construct a mathematically more elegant equation for the electron, which then led to the successful prediction of antimatter. "It is more important," he said, "to have beauty in one's equations than to have them fit experiment."[35]

Lisa Randall, a Harvard professor of theoretical particle physics and cosmology, in her *Knocking on Heaven's Door: How Physics and Scientific Thinking Illuminate the Modern World*, explains that the symmetries in the world are seldom perfect and often broken by changes in certain physical conditions. Echoing the perspective of Alfred North Whitehead on beauty, she writes:

> The theories that incorporate broken symmetries can be even more beautiful and interesting than those that are perfectly symmetrical. . . . After all, complete simplicity can be mind-numbing. When we look at art, we prefer something interesting that guides our eye. We want something simple enough to follow, but not so simple as to be boring. This seems to be how the world is constructed as well.[36]

As I discussed in chapter 2, it appears the universe was designed and fine-tuned for our benefit. Many physicists and cosmologists regard this fine-tuning as not only astonishing, but beautiful.[37] Some theologians see the hand of God in this fine-tuning, believing that it was God's plan from the beginning that mankind evolve and thrive.[38]

In summary, what modern physicists mean by "beauty" is seen, first of all, in the rationality, elegance, simplicity, and intricate interrelationship among nature's laws, and also, in the perfect symmetries that are found in nature and nature's laws. Understood in these terms, our universe is teeming with beauty. Because nature's laws are everywhere, beauty is everywhere and in everything. Perhaps we can apply these criterion for beauty to God—that is, that this beauty emanated from God's nature and that the propagation of such beauty is part of God's purpose.

34. Tegmark, *Our Mathematical Universe*, 266, 269.
35. Davies, *Mind of God*, 176.
36. Randall, *Knocking on Heaven's Door*, 267–68.
37. See, e.g., Rees, *Just Six Numbers*.
38. Polkinghorne, *Quarks, Chaos & Christianity*.

The Bonding Nature of Love

Let's now turn to love, assuming that it is also an aspect of God's purpose. We want to see if there are actually manifestations of love in the created world. But to do this, we have to know what we are looking for. Just as we sought to do with goodness and beauty, we need to conceptualize the essence of love. We need to start with that. Then we can see if it is borne out in the creation.

A foundational doctrine in Christian theology is that "God is love." This teaching is derived directly from Scripture (1 John 4:8). The text implies, however, that God is not literally love, but is loving . . . as demonstrated most dramatically in sending His only Son for mankind's redemption (1 John 4:9-10). Nonetheless, many theologians have posited that God's attributes (such as being a loving God) are identical with His essence; thus, God *is* love.[39] It would follow from this Christian teaching about God's nature that His purpose—a purpose that flows from His nature—would be the promulgation of love (as illustrated by His loving actions) throughout the universe.

In trying to conceptualize the essence of love, I do not want to rely on God's loving actions as revealed in Scripture. Our God is found in the depth of nature; He is not necessarily the God of Scripture or Christian theology. Nonetheless, the Christian teaching is consistent with what nature may reveal about God and love. In chapter 1, I said that the laws of physics, which emanated from God (in my view), seemed to manifest a *binding aspect* that came from God. Love is certainly a kind of bond, and the laws of physics certainly bind things together—like protons and neutrons to make a nucleus, a nucleus with electrons to make an atom, and the three quarks that make up a proton. This binding force is always bringing parts together to make wholes. Bonds prevail everywhere and in everything. Perhaps this tells us something about God's purpose, since this binding force ultimately emanated from His nature.

The concept of love as *bonding* is one of the ways philosophy, psychology, and literature have conceptualized love. There is no consensus about it, however. The philosophy of love has a long and varied history, dating back to pre-Socratic times.[40] There is also a long and varied history of love as portrayed and conceptualized in Western literature.[41] Love means different

---

39. See, e.g., Schleiermacher, *Christian Faith*, 730-32.

40. See, e.g., the masterful tour of this history in Irving Singer's trilogy: Singer, *Nature of Love*, vol. 1, *Plato to Luther*; vol. 2, *Courtly and Romantic*; vol. 3, *The Modern World*; and *Philosophy of Love: A Partial Summing-Up*.

41. Nussbaum, *Upheavals of Thought*, 457-710.

things to different people, and different historical periods have favored one conception of love over another.

Nonetheless, the concept of love as *bonding* is consistent with the approach we have been taking. I say that because bonds are so ubiquitous in the fundamental building blocks and forces in nature. We have already discussed many examples of this, such as the bonding power of the Strong Nuclear Force and how we might conceive of this as a manifestation of the bonding aspect of God's nature. Because this force is at work in the nucleus of every atom in the universe, it is not an exaggeration to say this aspect of God is *in* the world of nature as a sustaining power that enables everything to be what it is. Our awareness (thanks to quantum physics) of how these bonds are inherent in the fabric of nature helps us theologically as we endeavor to conceptualize God's nature and purpose. Insofar as these bonds manifest God's nature, we can infer that their ubiquity in nature manifests one aspect of His purpose. And insofar as we can justifiably call these bonds "love," we have a basis for seeing the propagation of love as part of His purpose.

Our first experience as infants with what could be called "love" is the bond and attachment we experience with our mothers or other such caregivers.[42] The bonding nature of love also applies to romantic love later in life. Many philosophers have also promoted the conceptualization of love as bonding.[43]

When we look at a mother nursing her infant, perhaps cooing sweetly to the baby, and see the infant gazing back at the mother, we think we are seeing love. But what *is* that? Aren't we seeing the manifestation of the *bond* and *attachment* between the mother and infant? These seem to be the perfect metaphors to capture what is occurring between them. There is also a neurobiological and molecular basis for what these metaphors convey.[44]

Literally, a bond is created by an adhesive between two surfaces, an adhesive that bonds the surfaces together. If we were to burn the object on one side of the bond, the other side would catch fire too, not because they are the same object, but because of the tight proximity between them. What happens to one side of the pair happens to the other.

The bond between the mother and infant is not literal, but nor is it merely a figure of speech. The bond is real but its nature is emotional. What happens to one *affects* the other, but does not literally happen to the other.

---

42. The 1900s brought watershed decades in psychoanalytic research and theory-building on parent-child attachment. This story is captured in Karen, *Becoming Attached*.

43. See, e.g., Nozick, "Love's Bond," 68–86.

44. See Keverne, "Neurobiological and Molecular Approaches."

If the infant falls out of its cradle and bumps her head, the mother does not have a bump as well, but the infant's fall affects the mother emotionally.

Literally, an attachment is created by a hitch of some kind between two objects. Train cars are attached to each other but not bonded together. Because they are attached, the motion of one car affects the motion of the others. Because they are not bonded, one car could catch fire without the blaze spreading to the adjacent car. In literal attachments between two objects, the effect that one side has on the other is usually the result of some kind of movement.

What is true of the bond between the mother and infant also applies to their attachment. It is not literal, but nor is it merely a figure of speech. Again, the attachment is real but its nature is emotional. If the mother leaves the room, the baby might cry or look anxious because of her attachment to her mother. If the baby is put down for a nap, the mother could miss her (that would be the emotional effect on the mother) because of their attachment.

These metaphors are also apt because bonds and attachments can vary in strength. Research has shown that toddlers can be *securely* attached to their mother, so that when the mother leaves the room, it registers a mild effect on the toddler, but the child does not throw a fit.[45] A toddler with a less secure attachment will show more anxiety when the mother leaves and act out its anxiety or anger when the mother returns.

If the bond or attachment between a romantic couple is strong, they are more likely to weather the storms between them. If a husband has a strong bond with his wife, and she has an affair, the emotional impact will be severe. The impact will be less traumatic if the couple is less strongly bonded or attached to each other.

In the philosophy of love, the metaphor "merging" has been used by some to capture the bond between romantic couples and between parents and children. Some philosophers believe this is exactly the wrong metaphor because people in love maintain their separate autonomy and sense of self.[46] Love, in their view, is the bond and attachment between autonomous selves.

While the metaphors "bond" and "attachment" may shed light on the essence of human love (between people, that is, as opposed to a person "loving" an opera), we are still left with our old conundrum about projecting this understanding of love onto God and His purpose. We should remember, however, that humans are part of God's creation; our nature is part of

---

45. Karen, *Becoming Attached*.
46. See, e.g., Singer, *Philosophy of Love*.

the world of nature as a whole. The nature of human love, therefore, may reveal something about the love that exists in the universe.

It can be argued that the nature of human love can be explained by evolution alone, without any reliance on nature as a whole or on the kind of naturalistic theology presented in this book. The bonds of love between parents and children, for example, have bestowed a survival advantage for the children. But why did nature bestow a *bond*; why not something else? Fear, for example, would have provided the motivation to stay close. A mother in Paleolithic times might have been so afraid of her child wandering off, causing shame and the burden of bearing a replacement child, that she held the child close to her and watched over the child . . . not lovingly, but fearfully. But human love does not seem to be made that way. It's an emotional bond, not a selfish fear.

My point is that the bonding nature of love may manifest a reality that is woven into the fabric of matter throughout the universe (as I mentioned earlier, in reference to the Strong Nuclear Force) and this reality may reflect as aspect of God's purposes. The binding and harmony-creating aspects that we have attributed to God's nature would support this conceptualization of His purpose.

I think we can conclude, from what we've seen in this chapter, that the concepts of goodness, beauty, and love are relevant to God's purposes. At least I believe it is reasonable to reach that conclusion. Whatever we *believe* about God's purposes will come down to just that . . . to our faith. But we want our faith to be informed with reason, and on that basis, I believe we can imagine God creating the universe to unleash the goodness, beauty, and love that were locked in His nature.

In our next chapter, we will explore what this could mean for us. Whitehead spoke of the "life of God" having a purpose, a life that is purpose-driven, we might add. We want our own lives to be purposeful too, and I want to think about how God's purposes could help us and how we could contribute to the life of God.

4

On Having a Purposeful Life

IN THE INTRODUCTION, I touched on nine troubling aspects of the human condition. Many of these pertained to our hunger for purpose and meaning, a hunger that can gnaw away at us because we want to matter, for our lives to have a lasting value or significance. Science falls silent in the face of this hunger. But our essential, vexing questions cannot be silenced. Why are we here? Will our lives matter in the long run? Is there a purpose to our existence? I said these questions were crying out to us for answers or at least a perspective to help us deal with them. And I promised that this book's theology would help in that regard. That is the task of the current chapter.

Mankind has grappled with questions of purpose and meaning for many centuries. We find ourselves here on this planet, with human bodies and human minds, and we know we did not create ourselves. By some means we came to be, but why? Philosophers, theologians, mystics, poets, novelists, shamans, and other religious thinkers have sought insight and wisdom about whether we are here for a reason and what that might be. In this chapter, we will tackle those questions in the following manner:

- We start with what we covered in the previous chapter about God's purposes in creating our world, suggesting that these purposes are a living, driving force in all of His creation.

- Because we are part of His creation, these purposes are our purposes too.
- Having a purposeful life is powered by the spirit of God that dwells within us.
- These purposes tell us why we are here and why and how we matter.
- We can also approach the question of why we are here by considering *what we are*. In this book's theology, we are manifestations of God's spirit.
- Our creation story said that God's purposes were not a *fait accompli*, that He is looking to us, and to all sentient beings, to help with the fulfillment of His purposes.

A Purposeful Universe

The story unfolding in this book seeks to imagine a God who created a purposeful universe—a universe that could bring about the fulfillment of His goodness, beauty, and love. Such purposes would be consistent with the God we sought to acquaint ourselves with through the book of nature. This was a good, beautiful, and loving God, as best we could determine.

I suggested that God's purposes became a living force in all of His creation. Everything is imbued with His purposes; they permeate every speck of matter and every spark of energy. They drive everything, in big ways and small, toward the goodness, beauty, and love that flowed from His nature. And yet the fulfillment of His purposes is not a done deal; it is a work in progress as the universe unfolds. I will return to this idea shortly.

Being Part of God's Creation

Because we are part of God's creation, we carry His purposes in our bones. Even if we do not know it or feel it, God's purposes are alive in us and define our purposes too. And if we can sense this, even if quietly and subtletly within us, then we can also sense what it means to live a purposeful life. God's purposes can inspire us, as a divine call from within. Each of us can make our thoughts and our actions more good, more beautiful, and more loving. We all know that; we can all do that.

This is how God's purposes speak to us. Our purposes, in a nutshell, are to enhance God's purposes by making our thoughts and actions as good, beautiful, and loving as we can.

God's Gift

Having a purposeful life does not come easily, especially in light of the misfortunes, traumas, and challenges life throws at us. Life is not a cakewalk for any of us. The problems we encounter can make it all but impossible to be increasingly good, beautiful, and loving.

And yet God is in us as the ground of our being (ch. 5), and this is the source of our power and resolve. God does not just call us toward His purposes; His presence in us is a never-ending resource for mastering the challenges of life. Even in the most trying and disquieting of circumstances, the God within us enables us to find some element, even if only a smattering, of goodness, beauty, and love. This is God's gift to us.

Why Are We Here? How Do We Matter?

If our purpose is to enhance God's purposes, as mentioned above, then we also know why we are here. And by contributing to those purposes, which are eternal, our lives gain a lasting, transcendent significance. This is how and why we matter.

The question of why we are here has been persistent and troubling over the course of human history. It starts, as I mentioned, with the startling realization of *finding ourselves here*, and yet knowing we did not put ourselves here or cause ourselves to be here. Our existence here feels caused by something outside ourselves. Finding ourselves here is a fundamental and foundational aspect of our experience and is the basis for the questions we are now considering. Because we are not self-caused, we have sought to understand the causes for our existence and whether there were reasons or purposes behind them.

It is often claimed that the question of why we are here is senseless; that there is no *why* in any objective or universal sense, only a *how*. Science can tell us how we got here, but nothing can answer the question of why with certainty.

This book's theology, however, offers an answer that science cannot. Because we are part of God's creation, a creation that has a purpose, then that purpose must certainly apply to us and offer a reason for our existence. We are here as emissaries of a divine cause—to make ourselves and our world evermore good, beautiful, and loving. This is God's call to us and His will *for* us.

It goes without saying that we want our lives to matter, to make a positive difference to a goal or cause that is important to us. As an obvious example, a goal that is important to most parents is the welfare of their children, and contributing to this goal is perhaps the most important way of having a life that matters. Such parents might also feel this is the purpose of their existence, to why they are here, in other words.

One problem with this approach is that most of the goals we have will ultimately pass away, which can make it seem that our mattering was short-lived. To return to the example of our children, their welfare is obviously important for their lives, but their lives will eventually end. The same can be said of other goals that are important to us: our personal accomplishments, for example, or making the world a better place, or the flourishing of our religious values and beliefs. None of these will matter a few centuries from now. Our sun and planet cannot last forever, and mankind itself will eventually come to an end. This is why we need a theology, in my view... a theology that speaks to a cause that transcends history.

In the theology of this book, we matter in a twofold sense: in the here and now, and at the same time, to the fulfillment of God's purposes in the long run. God's purposes can be *enhanced* in each instant of His creation. His purposes can only be *fulfilled* in the fullness of time, but this ultimate fulfillment builds on what occurs now, in each instant.

What Are We?

The question of why we are here can also be answered by knowing what we are. There is no obvious answer to this, as *what we are* can be conceptualized in different ways. Sticking with science alone, with no help from theology, we can define ourselves as human beings. That's what we are, and our purpose flows from that—namely, to survive and, if circumstances permit, to propagate our genes. This is the purpose wired into us by evolution.

It has been said that a chicken is the egg's way of making more eggs. Applying this to us, we can say that a human being is our genes' way of making more genes. If that is what we are, essentially, then our purpose becomes clear. The point of this example is that our self-definition (of what we are) contains the basis of our purpose.

We can also think of what we are in theological terms. One answer is that we are all *children of God*. That's what we are. It's a very powerful metaphor, as it speaks to our ultimate source and inheritance. We are *of God*, in that sense. His purposes have been bequeathed to us, to our innermost being.

Thinking of God as the ground of our being is another powerful metaphor. Plants grow out of the ground, just as we have grown from God. And plants manifest the potential in their seeds, just as we manifest God's nature. As we saw in chapter 1, there is a basis for seeing the basic building blocks of our bodies, and the basic forces that animate us and hold us together, as being *of God*. And if this is what we are, it defines our purpose and what it means to have a purposeful life.

I know I am beating this point to death, perhaps to better internalize what it means to have a purposeful life in the long run. I suppose I want you to be grasped by this was well.

Enhancing God's Purposes

I mentioned above that God's purposes for His creation are a work in progress and that we can contribute to its fulfillment by making our thoughts and our actions evermore good, beautiful, and loving. This is a radical theological notion because it implies that God's purposes are not a *fait accompli*. It challenges a basic tenet in theology and in every religion—namely, that God's will is being done and indeed *will* be done by the end of time. This is referred to as God's *providence* or as God's providential rule over the universe. Everything that happens is in accordance with His will. Thus, if God wills goodness, beauty, and love in His creation, it would be silly to suggest that we can contribute to or impede their fulfillment.

Regarding God's providential rule, the definition given by the theologians Karl Rahner and Herbert Vorgrimler can be paraphrased as follows:

> Divine providence is God's plan for the created world, based on his knowledge and will, his wisdom and love. It mightily sustains and controls all things. This plan even embraces human freedom (without destroying it), and by it God in his eternity guides the course of the world and its history . . . to the goal he has foreseen and predestined.[1]

God is in charge, in other words, and His jurisdiction encompasses the entire universe and every event therein. His plan for the world will be evident and completed when the story of the universe reaches its end. This is a theology that makes God's purposes for the universe a forgone conclusion. He certainly does not need our help in accomplishing His goals.

In the history of theology, God is not only in charge; He also has all the resources within His nature to accomplish His purposes. He is omnipotent and omniscient, and perfect in justice, love, and goodness. Our stature and power, by comparison, are abysmally insignificant. It can seem outlandish

---

1. Rahner and Vorgrinler, "Divine Providence," 390.

to think we can enhance God's purposes or that we were called by our inner God to do so.

Let's take a closer look at these issues.

The Question of God's Dominion

The God of the Old Testament is most certainly an almighty God who has dominion over His kingdom. In fact, He is acclaimed as such in the first line of the Christian creed: I believe in God, the Father Almighty. We do not know, however, if this was the God Jesus believed in. In the version of the Lord's Prayer passed down to us, Jesus taught his apostles to pray that God's "will be done, on earth as it is in heaven." It seems that Jesus believed that God's will automatically prevailed in heaven, *but not necessarily on earth.* That was something that we needed to pray for.

Since God's omnipotence is such a prevalent aspect of religious belief, it may seem audacious to suggest that our God—the God we are trying to get to know in this book, with the method we are employing—may not have dominion over everything that happens in His creation. The sacred texts of most religions are thought to be divinely inspired and to contain the revelation of God to man. And God is revealed to be all-powerful. But we are looking at the book of nature to see what it reveals about God. So if we stick to that approach, we have to ask: Does the natural world itself point to the omnipotence of the creator?

Certainly our method would attribute to God *enough* power to bring the universe into being. But God would not need to be all-powerful to accomplish this goal; He only needs to be powerful *enough*. Some theologians hold that the omnipotence of God means that He possess the sum total of all the power that could possibly exist. Thus, there is no leftover power to be used independently by the forces of nature or by sentient beings that were to evolve and possess free will (a kind of power of their own).

This book's theology posits that God is *not* all-powerful, for the following reasons:

1. As I mentioned above, there is a logical reason for God to be powerful *enough* to create the universe but no logical reason for Him to be all-powerful.

2. A less than all-powerful God is a God that we can more easily adore and want to help. This God needs the participation of all conscious beings everywhere to bring about His purposes. An all-powerful God would not need us in this way.

3. A less than all-powerful God cannot be blamed for the evil in the world and for all the bad things that happen to good people. Instead, he would suffer with us and want to help in all the ways available to Him. I will return to this theme in chapter 6.

4. A less than all-powerful God possesses an awesome and profound courage that we can admire and seek to emulate. The creation was a risky proposition on God's part because He knew there was no guarantee that His lofty purposes would be achieved.

5. The God in this book's theology did not create His own nature, and He found a lack of omnipotence there, as well as random forces that could sabotage His purposes. He nonetheless let His creation spring forth, believing and trusting that His purposes would prevail. This is a cause that all sentient beings, including us, can foster.

This approach to the question of God's power also applies to His knowledge. He had to know *enough* to make a responsible decision about creating the universe. He had to know His own nature, the laws of physics that would emanate from His nature, and the likely outcome of these laws as the universe unfolded. But He could not know the consequences of the random, unpredictable forces in His nature. Knowing the future, even for God, was not possible or necessary.

Our discussion in chapter 1 about causal determinism and randomness is relevant here. In a perfect universe ruled by causal determinism, the goodness, beauty, and love of the first cause (God) would lead to effects that were *only* good, beautiful, and loving. But random forces would throw a wrench in the works. We surmised that God was aware of this problem before the act of creation. He would have known, perhaps painfully so, that His power was limited and that He would not be able to *prevent* unplanned and untoward consequences in his creation.

We are left then with a universe with mixed, competing forces; the forces of goodness vs. the forces of evil, if you will. This implies a stark question for the human race—that is, does our goodness outweigh our potential for evil? The late philosopher Robert Nozick was thinking about this when he took up the question of mankind's value, asking whether it was good that the human race evolved. In his mind, the Holocaust was such a devastating indictment of human nature that he wondered if it would have been better had mankind never evolved, given the potential for savagery that is embedded in our nature.[2]

2. Nozick, "Holocaust," 236–42.

God's Call to Us

Because the fulfillment of God's purposes is a work in progress, if you will, beings like us that exist in His creation can make a meaningful difference. Perhaps we can hear in this a call from God, a call from the ground of our being to do our part. And this is how our lives can have a lasting or transcendent meaning. This is how our lives can be meaningful to God and honor God.

Many of the ways our lives are meaningful are transitory. Our meaning can be anchored in our own lives, the lives of our loved ones, or the contribution we make to the larger society or culture. But these sources of meaning will someday cease to exist. If we feel we haven't wasted our lives, that we have loved and been loved, for example, then after we die, the question can be posed: What happened to the meaning we created? I am afraid that it will have died with us if it only existed in our minds.

But suppose this meaning did not only exist in our minds; suppose it made a contribution to God's eternal purposes and is held close in the heart of God for all time? This could be true of every good, beautiful, or loving thing we do, whether in our thoughts only or also in the actions we take. Even if we regret that we have not accomplished more, this regret is based on the essential goodness within us and is gratefully accepted in the divine order. Even if we regret the shallowness of our character, this regret also is taken into the heart of God because it says something beautiful about us.

I recently read a diary of a Holocaust victim (a diary discovered after the war) who wrote that he and his fellow Jews had chosen to face their deaths with resolute courage and without resistance because any resistance whatsoever was met with savage reprisals toward other Jews. In solidarity with the plight of Jews everywhere, they were choosing not to make matters worse. They would recite the Kaddish as they faced the mass grave before them, knowing they were about to take a bullet to the back of their skulls. What good did this do? Regarding the fate of the Jews under Nazi rule, it probably made no difference since the wholesale slaughter never let up. But perhaps it made a difference to God's purposes because it helped to balance the evil that was occurring with something good—solidarity, resolve, and the intention of saving others.

God's Dilemma Harkens to Us

In thinking of our role in enhancing God's purposes, and in thinking of a purposeful life in that context, it can be helpful to imagine the dilemma that God was facing before creating our world. On the one hand, God was aware of the goodness, beauty, and love in His nature, and He was aware of the laws of physics (including those pertaining to causal determinism) that would emanate from His nature. On this basis, He could envision a creation that would be good, beautiful, and loving. On the other hand, He was aware of the random forces in His nature that could, once they took flight in His creation, impede the fulfillment of His purposes and cause chaos and evil. He therefore had to weigh the pros and cons before letting His nature burst forth and create our world. We can imagine He believed that His goodness, beauty, and love would prevail over disorder and evil, and that He created the universe on that basis. But He could not *guarantee* this outcome; it rested on what He *believed* would result in His creation.

Had God not believed and trusted in these things, He would have held back and let nonbeing prevail, for at least it would have been safer. Had he held back, I believe His reasons would have come down to the dictum: Do no harm.

The dilemma God was facing back then, and His boldness in creating our world, harkens now to each of us, calling us to advance His goodness, beauty, and love. God's belief that His purposes would prevail can now be seen as His belief in us. He believed that beings such as us would do our part.

The importance of our role in enhancing His purposes becomes clear when we see the chaotic forces that must be overcome. Looking at our own planet, we can see the havoc wrought by the chaotic randomness that impedes God's purposes. Think of all the deadly and crippling diseases we are vulnerable to. Think of all the children born with horrible mental or bodily defects. Think of the viruses and infections that can overwhelm our immune system. Think of all the mental illnesses we are subject to, and think of the disintegration of our brains and minds that afflict so many of us in old age. These examples barely scratch the surface of the suffering that comes from being human. We suffer this way because of the disruption of orderly processes caused by random mutations, random infections, or the random disintegration that affects some minds. Our bodies and minds are vulnerable to random chaos in our cells.

Of course, if a tally could be done of all the randomly-caused suffering in our world, alongside a tally of all the love, health, and happiness in our world, perhaps the verdict would be in our favor, that overall, God's purposes are thriving here.

Earlier, I mentioned the call from God that is ever-present, coming from the Ground of our Being, even though we may not hear it or know it. This God is driven by His purposes, and we can be driven by His purposes too. We can step back from ourselves and take stock of the mixture of traits that have evolved in us. We can do all we can to harness the good in us so that it prevails over our negative tendencies. And when we are battered by life, the God within us is there to provide the inner strength we need to endure the slings and arrows of our misfortune.

In chapter 6, I will discuss the notion of God's sorrow for our suffering. The degree of physical pain our bodies can experience is a result of the disorder in the natural world. There is no reason for our pain to be as horrible as it is, and at such times, it is impossible to be thinking of God's purposes.

We are manifestations of God. That's where we find the truth of our existence, and where we find the meaning of a purposeful life. It is a cliché to refer to "the grand scheme of things," but this expression points to a divine order in the universe, a divine intention toward goodness, beauty, and love. The human order in which we live is not the whole story; there is a larger context in which we live, a divine order that gives meaning to our lives. In his classic study of religious experience, William James found that belief in such an order was *the* most common characteristic of religious faith.[3]

---

3. James, *Varieties of Religious Experience*.

5

The Theology of Paul Tillich

God as the Ground of Our Being

OUR LAST CHAPTER INCLUDED a remembrance of WWII Jews facing a mass grave, about to be shot in the back of their heads, all the while refusing to resist or protest in order to prevent Nazi reprisals on their fellow Jews who were still in camp. We have to ask: What was the source of their goodness and courage? This is where the theology of Paul Tillich comes into our story. God was within these Jews as the Ground of their Being, the innermost source of what they needed to face death resolutely and prevent greater torture or cruelty for Jews who were still imprisoned.

God as the innermost source of our goodness speaks to the immanence of God as opposed to His transcendence. Both these concepts are found in the history of theology. In His transcendence, He is thought to be *above and beyond* His creation as an eternal and watchful divine being. In His immanence, He is *within* His creation, and therefore within us. The Latin root of this concept of immanence is that God "dwells within" His creation.

Our speculation about the God from the book of nature gives a *scientific* grounding to the immanence of God. The Strong Nuclear Force, for example, dwells within every atom in the universe. This force manifests the immanence of God because it is essentially *of God*, in the sense that God is the source of this force and because it expresses the binding aspect of God's nature.

Paul Tillich, on the other had, offers a *theological* grounding to the immanence of God. In his theology, God dwells within all things as the Ground of Being and dwells within us as the Ground of *our* Being. As I mentioned in chapter 1, we might prefer the metaphor *glue* of our being in light of the Strong Nuclear Force, as this force is the glue that binds together the proton and neutron within every atom of every cell of our bodies. Tillich's metaphor, *ground* of our being, is nearly identical in its meaning. Particle physics (in the interpretation I offered in chapter 1) and Tillich's theology agree that we owe our being to God.

What particle physics cannot tell us, however, is how owing our being to God is of any help to us. That's why I am devoting a chapter to Paul Tillich.

Paul Tillich was born in 1886 in a small German village where his father was a conservative Lutheran pastor. He earned his doctorate of philosophy at the University of Breslau in 1911 and his licentiate of theology degree at the University of Halle-Wittenberg in 1912. Also in 1912, Tillich was ordained as a Lutheran minister. He served as a chaplain in the Imperial German Army during WWI. After the war he held many prestigious academic appointments in German universities. In the early 1930s he was critical of the growing Nazi movement, which cost him his job at the University of Frankfurt. A famous colleague, Reinhold Niebuhr, helped him obtain a position at New York City's Union Theological Seminary. He taught there from 1933 to 1955, and also held positions at Columbia, the Harvard Divinity School, and the University of Chicago Divinity School. He died in Chicago in 1965.

During WWII, Tillich made numerous broadcasts over Radio Free Europe urging his fellow Germans to resist Nazism.

Tillich has authored numerous highly-acclaimed books over the course of his career[1] and is widely regarded as one of the most influential theologians of the twentieth century.[2] He was both an existential philosopher and Christian theologian. In keeping with the existential tradition, he was relentless and fearless when it came to laying bare the harsh realities of the human condition. As a theologian, he developed a theology that confronted these realities head-on; in his view, these were the questions theology must answer.[3]

We can see the relevance of Tillich's God, as the Ground of our Being, in the example I gave in the precious chapter of concentration camp

---

1. For a scholarly overview of Tillich's life, his most notable books, and the main tenants of his theology, see Kelsey, *Fabric of Paul Tillich's Theology*.

2. Braaten and Jenson, *Map of Twentieth-Century Theology*.

3. Tillich, *Systematic Theology*, 61.

prisoners who did not resist their execution, as doing so would bring horrendous reprisals against other Jews. This would not have been humanly possible, in Tillich's view, without the power coming from the God within.

The Threat of Meaninglessness

It is also the God within that undergirds our response to the threat of meaninglessness. The meaninglessness of human existence is a dominant theme in existential philosophy. It goes like this: Life is meaningless because nothing ultimately lasts and nothing ultimately matters. The transitory nature of our existence, and of those who matter to us, ruins everything. The meaning we create dies with us and with our loved ones. Whatever we accomplish in life is lost and forgotten forever, and if we like to think we have made a difference for mankind as a whole, we should remember that all of humanity and everything mankind has accomplished will be lost and forgotten forever when the solar system is obliterated by our exploding sun.

Tillich's theology does not deny any of this or seek to sugarcoat it. Nor does he run from it. He meets it head-on. The God of the Bible, he reasons, must be a God that can address this problem. Otherwise we have an irrelevant and useless God.

The problem of meaninglessness, in Tillich's view, is the *threat* that it poses.[4] It can threaten our desire to live, and it can threaten the sense of fulfillment that we want from life. Our human response to this threat can go one of two ways, both of which pertain to the deal we are offered by life. The deal is this: we get to live, but we have to die, and having to die obliterates all meaning. We can say *no* to life, that we do not accept the deal. If nothing matters, then why bother living? The existential writer Albert Camus said that suicide is the main philosophical question.[5] Should we accept the absurdity of wanting meaning when there is none, or is it more dignified, from a human standpoint, to take our own life in protest?

The other human response is to say *yes* to life *in spite of* its meaninglessness. Tillich does not mean that we would say: Who cares if life has no meaning, I still enjoy living. No, Tillich wants us to say: I deplore the meaninglessness of life, but life is good *in spite of* it. It is good to be a mortal creature. Even if it has no meaning, life is still worth living. Even if we are fated to a meaningless existence, life is still good. He wants us to accept and affirm life on its own terms.

4. The following discussion is drawn from Tillich, *Courage to Be*, 46–50, 167–78.
5. Camus, *Myth of Sisyphus*.

Then Tillich turns to two rather jolting questions: Where do we get the *courage* to face up to things the way they are—to face up to the fact that nothing ultimately matters—and where do we get the *spunk* to affirm life's goodness in spite of it having no meaning? Tillich believes that the God within us is the source of this courage and this spunk.[6]

This is an example of how Tillich's mind works. You may not agree with his conclusions about meaninglessness,[7] but notice what he has done. First, he takes on a problem that is inherent in the human condition. The problem is the transitory nature of our existence and how it can rob our life of ultimate meaning. Second, he thinks about optimal ways of dealing with the problem—ways of responding to it that are built on the courage and tenacity of the human spirit. And he sees that many of us actually do respond in those ways, and he believes all of us are capable of it. Then he thinks about God, believing that God is at the core of our being and must be able to help us, if he is at all useful or relevant to our existential situation. Finally, he reasons that God does help us by being the *source* of our courage and tenacity. That's where this courage and tenacity come from in the first place. And that's where he sees the power of God working in us, the power of the ground of our being.

The Ground of our Being

Since the time of Plato, philosophers have grappled with the problem of being. Nothing just exists without a substance that makes it what it is. Things do not just exist; they are *being* what they are. This is called the beingness of things. But what is it that *enables* things to be what they are? They must possess the power to be that thing, which Tillich calls "the power of being." Where does the power of being come from?

Now, if you think this is a problem that only philosophers would dream up and waste time on, consider your own beingness. You are not just a creature; you are a human *being*. That's one aspect of your beingness, an aspect that defines your basic nature. But you are also *being* the unique person you are. That's another aspect of your beingness, an aspect that defines your individual essence. You are not just a creature and you are not a non-person. These aspects of your beingness have a source. It's a source with the power to create your beingness. That's why it's called the power of being.

---

6. On Tillich's theology of courage, see Tillich, *Courage*, 155–90, and Tillich, *Systemic*, 189, 194–95, 273–74.

7. I, for one, do not agree because our lives can make a contribution to God's eternal cause and be ultimately meaningful in that sense (see ch. 3, p. 129).

THE THEOLOGY OF PAUL TILLICH   77

Tillich belongs to the philosophical tradition that has grappled with the question: where does the power of being come from?[8] It cannot come from another being, because then the question would be: where does the power of *its* being come from? Plato's answer is that every being partakes of the power and essence of Being Itself. This essence informs every specific being; it is their common denominator. Being Itself is not another being; it is the essence of all beingness.

Tillich's answer is that God is the Ground of Being.[9] God is the source, substance, and sustainer of all being. God is within everything, giving all things the power to be . . . first of all, the power to be something as opposed to nothing, and thus to have the *general* state of beingness, and secondly, the power to be the *specific*, unique thing that it is.

If we go back to our discussion of the Planck Era, comprising the initial conditions that exploded in the big bang, we imagined that these conditions were the primordial manifestation of God's nature. We then turned to the metaphysical notion of Being to ask: What enabled these conditions *to be* what they were? The answer was that they had to be the source and ground of their own being, since no other being existed at the time. In other words, we were thinking of God as the ground of His own being. I wanted to review these points because they are so relevant to Tillich's view of God. Starting as the ground of His own being, God became the ground of all being in the act of creation.

Tillich does not say *how* God is the source, substance, and sustainer of all being. Our discussion of the book of nature, however, helps to answer this question. The book of nature is scientific: it describes the fundamental building blocks of matter and the fundamental forces that operate at the quantum level. Theology enters the picture when we consider the ultimate source of these building blocks and forces and what they reveal about this source. This is where we meet God. This is the science behind Tillich's theology.

If God is the ground of all being, it goes without saying that He is the ground of our being too. Again, the metaphor "ground," in Tillich's theology, includes the notion of source, substance, and sustainer. Ultimately, we come from God, as everything does. The deepest substance of our being is *of God*. Every second of our lives, we are sustained by God in our beingness, and in being who we are.

---

8. Tillich, *Systematic*, 189, 230–31, 235–57, 272–73.

9. Tillich's theology about God, as the Ground of Being, is presented in Tillich, *Systemic*, pt. 2, 211–89, and esp. 155–58, 235, 238, 284.

Confronting Anxiety and the Threat of Despair

Tillich is primarily interested, I believe, in how God—as the ground of our being—can help us in dealing with our existential situation and the unavoidable anxiety that it throws at us. In *The Courage to Be*, Tillich discusses the many types of anxiety that are endemic in the human condition.

We are anxious about having to die. This includes our anxiety about how we will die and the suffering of mind and body that it could entail, and it includes our anxiety about no longer existing (what Tillich calls nonbeing). "For existentially everybody is aware of the complete loss of self that biological extinction implies."[10] We can run from this anxiety, but there is no hiding from it. We can rationalize that it will not be so bad, or that "what will be, will be," so that there is no reason to fret about it. These walls of denial and repression that we build against the anxiety of death help quiet the anxiety but do not subdue it.

We are anxious about our fate and the contingent nature of our existence. Ultimately everything is beyond our control. We do not control the time of our birth or the time of our death. We do not control what happens in the world and in the historical period in which we find ourselves. We do not control our gender or the characteristics of our bodies. We do not control the nature of our personality. We do not control the gifts and aspirations, or the shortcomings of character, that we find in ourselves. We do not control the most significant events in our lives. All of these things are the givens of our existence.

Earlier, I discussed the threat of meaninglessness. We are anxious about that too. As Tillich writes, "The anxiety of meaninglessness is anxiety about the loss of an ultimate concern, of a meaning which gives meaning to all meanings. This anxiety is aroused by the loss of a spiritual center, of an answer, however symbolic and indirect, to the question of the meaning of existence."[11] It is an anxiety that can leave us feeling empty.

We are anxious about the fact that we do not live up to our potential and we do not abide by our own values and ideals. We know the truth about ourselves and feel guilty for falling short, and we find it impossible to fully accept and love ourselves. "Man's being," Tillich writes, "is not only given to him but demanded of him. He is responsible for it; literally, he is required to answer, if he is asked, what he has made of himself."[12] We ask this question of ourselves and judge ourselves accordingly.

---

10. Tillich, *Courage to Be*, 42.
11. Tillich, *Courage to Be*, 47.
12. Tillich, *Courage to Be*, 51.

These anxieties can cause us to despair of life, and oftentimes they do. But Tillich's point is this: These anxieties do not cause despair in all of us, at least not all the time. And the question is, why don't they? His answer is not a psychological defense mechanism, such as denial, that keeps these anxieties at bay and provides a safe harbor from despair. His answer is much deeper than that, going to the very core of our being. That's where God is, the ground of our being, giving us the inner resources to hold our own against these anxieties. We are made of God, and where God is, there also is the courage to take these anxieties on and claim the promise of a fulfilling life in spite of the anxieties that afflict us.

On Being Estranged

I mentioned earlier that Tillich wants to show how God, as the ground of our being, can help us in dealing with the downsides of being human. *He believes the ground of our being is also the call of our being, calling us to lay claim to the power that comes from the God within us.* Our human nature is a mixed bag, Tillich believes; it has given rise to the saints among us, and to the monsters among us as well. The power from God is the power to resist and transcend the forces of darkness within us and the power to allow the better angels of our nature to come forth. We see this in Tillich's analysis of sin and grace.[13]

Tillich believes that sin is the state in which we find ourselves; sin is not something that we commit but is the state we are in. We exist in a state of estrangement from each other, from ourselves, and from the ground of our being. This estrangement is our sinful state. Grace, on the other hand, is that power from within that overcomes estrangement and *reunites* us with each other, *reconciles* us with ourselves, and allows us to be grasped by the ground of our being. What is Tillich talking about here? I could try to summarize Tillich's answer to this question, but his own words are more powerful and cutting to the truth.

On our estrangement from each other, Tillich writes:

> Who has not, at some time, been lonely in the midst of a social event? Our feeling of separation from the rest of life is most acute when we are surrounded by it in noise and talk. We realize then much more than in moments of solitude how strange we are to each other, how estranged life is from life.... We cannot penetrate the hidden center of another individual, nor can that individual pass beyond the shroud that covers our own being.

13. The following discussion is based on Tillich, *Shaking of the Foundations*, 153–63.

> ... [There is] a hidden hostility in the ground of our souls. We can confirm what Immanuel Kant, the prophet of human reason and dignity, was honest enough to say: there is something in the misfortune of our best friends that does not displease us. Who among us is dishonest enough to deny that this is true also of him?[14]

When Tillich says we cannot penetrate the hidden center of another individual, I think he means that we cannot know what it is like to be this other individual. This point applies, I believe, even to our loved ones—to our spouses or children, for example—with whom we feel the closest of bonds. We might feel that we know them inside and out, but if the truth be known, we really do not know *what it is like to be* some other person, to fully know what their lived experience is like from the inside.

Tillich goes on to write about our response to the suffering of our fellow humans around the world:

> Let us consider ourselves what we feel, when we read, this morning and tonight, that in some sections of Europe all children under the age of three are sick and dying, or that in some sections of Asia millions without homes are freezing and starving to death. The strangeness of life to life is evident in the strange fact that we can know all this, and yet can live today, this morning and tonight, as if we were completely ignorant. And I refer to the most sensitive people among us. In both mankind and nature, life is separated from life. Estrangement prevails among all things that live.[15]

On our estrangement from ourselves, Tillich describes the hidden hostility and contempt we experience toward ourselves because of our inherent self-centeredness and our failure to live up to our values and ideals. He believes the power of self-sabotage resides in each of us. Commenting on what the Apostle Paul wrote, Tillich says:

> Nothing is more obvious than the split between our unconscious life and our conscious personality. Without the help of modern psychology, Paul expressed the fact in his famous words: "For I do not do the good I desire, but rather the evil that I do not desire." And then he continued with words that might be the motto of all depth psychology: "Now if I do what I do not wish to do, it is not I that do it, but rather sin which dwells within me." The apostle sensed a split between his conscious will and

---

14. Tillich, *Shaking of the Foundations*, 157.
15. Tillich, *Shaking of the Foundations*, 158.

his real will, between himself and something strange within and alien to him. He was estranged from himself, and that estrangement he called "sin."[16]

The reason we are estranged from each other and from ourselves is this:

> Because we are estranged from the ground of our being, because we are estranged from the aim and origin of our life. We do not know where we have come from and we do not know where we are going. We are separated from the mystery, the depth, and the greatness of our existence. We hear the voice of that depth, but our ears are closed. We feel that something total, radical, and unconditioned is demanded of us, but we rebel against it, try to escape its urgency, and will not accept its promise.[17]

Where is God in all this? How can the ground of our being help? Tillich's answer is that God provides the grace we need, which is the *power of reconciliation* . . . with our fellow humans, with ourselves, and with the ground of our being. Tillich does not believe we can make this happen. Rather, it is given to us. We are grasped by it. This has already happened to each of us, although we were unaware of it. And this tends to happen, Tillich believes, at those times when we are most in need of the transforming power of grace. Somehow the God within us knows what we need and when we need it, and offers this up as a free gift.

Here is a commonplace example that most of us can relate to. We can all think of times when we had an argument with a friend, or with our spouse, an argument that created a wall of separation between us. Then suddenly we found ourselves letting go of our own self-righteous position and instead of that, we were now listening as carefully as we possibly could in order to understand, to really understand, the other person's point of view on the issue that came between us. Had we been asked, we would have been able to articulate this opposing point of view as if it were our own. That's how intently we had listened and tried to grasp the validity of this opposing viewpoint. And we found the wall between us melting away as if by magic. But it wasn't magic, it was the ground of our being offering up what we needed just then. It was the gift of grace, with no strings attached. The God within us, Tillich believes, is not a manipulative or coercive God. He respects our right to say *no* to Him, as He is also the ground of our autonomy.

---

16. Tillich, *Shaking of the Foundations*, 159.
17. Tillich, *Shaking of the Foundations*, 159.

Tillich believes that one of the most transformative ways we are rescued by the ground of our being concerns our negative feelings about ourselves. If we were truly and fearlessly honest with ourselves, we would admit that we do not *deserve* the love and admiration that comes our way. This is because, in Tillich's view, of our failure to live up to our own values and ideals, as I mentioned earlier. Not being deserving of love and admiration causes us to disparage or devalue the positive feelings that others have toward us. It's as if we are saying to ourselves: If only they knew the real truth about me, they would not hold me in such esteem. Or we might do things that could cause others to withdraw their love and admiration.

The God within us, however, loves and accepts us as we are. He knows the real truth about us and sees every flaw in our character. But He knows that we did not choose to have these shortcomings and He accepts us in spite of them. The grace that God offers us is the grace of self-acceptance, to feel the same compassion toward ourselves that God does, to accept ourselves as God does. As Tillich writes:

> And in the light of this grace . . . we experience moments in which we accept ourselves because we feel we have been accepted by that which is greater than we. If only more such moments were given to us! For it is such moments that make us love life, that make us accept ourselves, not in our goodness or self-complacency, but in our certainty of the eternal meaning of our life. We cannot force ourselves to accept ourselves. . . . But sometimes it happens that we receive the power to say "yes" to ourselves, that peace enters into us and makes us whole, that self-hate and self-contempt disappear, and that our self is reunited with itself. Then we can say that grace has come into us.[18]

The Source of Grace and Sin

You might recall from chapter 1 that we hypothesized competing forces within God's nature—a bonding force that pulled things together (such as the attraction of neutrons and protons within the nucleus of atoms) and a repulsive force that pushed things apart (such as all particles with the same electric charge). Although Tillich does not refer to these forces, his analysis of grace and sin is very consistent with them. Grace is that which binds us to the better angels we carry inside, to our fellow humans, and to the Ground of our Being. And sin is that which creates separation and

---

18. Tillich, *Shaking of the Foundations*, 163.

alienation. These competing forces may be manifestations of the dialectic within God's nature.

In philosophy, the concept of "dialectic" refers to the interplay of competing forces or dynamics. This interplay is thought to be imbedded in nature itself, in human nature, and in social and political history. Tillich's analysis of grace and sin is dialectical because these forces operate over against each other. When grace abounds, sin is diminished; when sin takes over, grace fades into the background (but is never completely destroyed).

In chapter 2, when we considered God's aim in bringing the universe into being, we speculated that He was aware of the dialectic within His nature—the dialectic between bonding and repulsive forces—but that He knew or hoped the bonding forces would win out. In Tillich's theology, God believed that grace would overpower sin as the universe unfolded. The notion that sin, as a force that keeps things apart, comes from God's nature may offend some believers because it implies an imperfection in God. You might recall from chapter 1, however, that the repulsive forces between like charges may serve God's purpose by keeping *incompatible* particles apart. Thus, these forces would not imply an imperfection in God. But these forces could also give rise to the estrangement that Tillich regards as sinful, although Tillich (as I mentioned) believed that grace would have the upper hand.

I am mentioning all this to make a point that I believe Tillich would want me to make. Grace is not preordained to have the upper hand. It is a force within us, coming from the Ground of our Being, a force *that calls us* to embrace it and bring it forth. When we heed that call, we lessen the suffering that sin causes, but we also contribute to the fulfillment of God's purposes.

Tillich wants us to appreciate that grace is a power within us that can soothe the suffering caused by sin. This is the suffering of loneliness, despair, and helplessness . . . a suffering that makes illness, injury, or abuse all the more difficult to bear. Tillich beckons us to call forth the grace that abides within us, but in the final analysis, the most we can do is open our hearts to the power of grace and allow ourselves to be grasped by this power. As Tillich puts it:

> We cannot find it, but it can find us. It tries to find us during our whole life, and then suddenly we are grasped by it. . . . We cannot transform our lives unless we allow them to be transformed by that stroke of grace. It strikes us when we are in great pain and restlessness. It strikes us when we feel our life is meaningless and empty, or when we feel our separation is deeper than

usual because we have violated another life, a life that we loved or from which we were estranged. It strikes us when our disgust for our indifference, our weakness, or hostility, and our lack of direction and composure have become intolerable to us.[19]

Let me offer an example of what the power of grace can do when we need it most. Suppose you have a child who is killed in an accident or from a fatal disease. If you could, you would ask Tillich how you could possibly endure the pain of this loss. Here is what he would say. You can endure this pain by knowing your child's life was worth living and that your pain in losing this child is not so inconsolable as to cause you to condemn life itself. You can affirm the goodness of life and the blessing of having this child in your life *in spite of* your pain and *in spite of* your child's death. You can be grateful for having this child in spite of your loss, a loss that your gratitude helps you to endure. This affirmation of life and this gratitude for what life has given you come from God, from the power in the Ground of your Being. In the final analysis, it is only this affirmation and gratitude that can help you, and this is exactly the help that the God within you gives.

In Tillich's view, the God within us does not cancel out our suffering, but He can give us what we need to suffer less. We need to feel that we are not ultimately alone. We need to feel that we are in God's loving hands. We need to know there is a point to life. We need to know that we can find help—from within ourselves and from others. All this help comes from grace, from our union with the God within.

The Aim and Origin of Our Life

I will close this chapter by referring again to Tillich's notion that we are estranged from the Ground of our Being, *from the aim and origin of our life*. I believe there is something enormously compelling and profound in the idea that our life has an aim and origin that we cannot fully know or fully grasp, and yet the aim and origin of our life can grasp us in moments of searing need. In such moments, we can pray to be grasp by what we truly are, a prayer that calls forth the power of the God within us.

In his sermon on the meaning of joy,[20] Tillich explains that the aim of our life is found in the joy that comes from God. God's joy comes from the fulfillment of the potential that abounds in His creation. Everything in God's creation is *of God*—coming from God and carrying His purposes.

---

19. Tillich, *Shaking of the Foundations*, 100, 161.
20. Tillich, "Meaning of Joy," 141–51.

God is joyful when His purposes are fulfilled. We share in this joy when we fulfill the potential bequeathed to us, allowing the ground of our being to shine through. In Tillich's theology, fulfilling this potential is the true aim of our life and the source of transforming joy, of God's joy, actually.

6

A Personal God?

WHILE TILLICH'S GOD IS a personal God, he believes it is problematic to assert that God is a person.[1] And the God we are getting to know in this book, as revealed initially in the book of nature, is not obviously a person or even a personal God. This is a central issue for the theology we are developing. We can approach it intellectually or theoretically, but it also has an emotional component. Intellectually, we want to explore whether it makes sense to attribute personhood to the God revealed by the book of nature. Emotionally, we *want* this to make sense. Most of us who believe in God *want* that God to be a person and *want* a personal relationship with Him. But wanting these things does not make them so. We have to think these matters through to see if a personal God makes sense.

Here are the questions I want us to consider in this chapter. Is there a basis for attributing a kind of personhood to God or for actually thinking of Him as a person? Moreover, on what basis is He a divine person who dwells within us and cares about us? Does it make sense to be personally devoted to this God? Does it make sense to pray to this God or worship this God?

I think we should admit that the God we imagined from the book of nature is not *directly* revealed to be a personal God. By "personal God," I

---

1. Tillich, *Systemic Theology*, 245.

mean a God who is a person or at least has the semblance of personhood, in line with our human conception of what it means to be a person. It would also be a God with whom humans can feel a person-to-person relationship.

Nature's revelation of God as personal is indirect and by inference. It points to a God who has personal characteristics. It is a God who, before the creation, engaged in person-like mental activities. He had *to envision* the kind of universe that would emanate from His nature. To do this, He had *to know* His nature. He had *to decide* whether to create the universe. Presumably, in my view, He had *to weigh* the pros and cons. He had *to will* the universe into being. He *acted* as a creative agent. These are all things that are done by persons, which is why I referred to them as person-like activities.

In addition to these activities, the notion that God has purposes (as discussed in chapter 3) implies that He also possesses person-like *sentiments*. He *intends* and *hopes* that His purposes will be fulfilled. Presumably, He also *cares* about the well-being of His creation and sentient beings such as us. Because of His purposes, He is not indifferent to what happens. And because He cares, He would also experience something akin to what humans mean by *emotional states*. He would feel pleased, for example, or even happy or joyful, if His purposes were being fulfilled. (We reviewed Tillich's perspective on God's joy in the previous chapter.) He would feel sorrow if this were not the case. We speculated in chapter 1 about a possible meaning of the concept *God is love*. Having emotions about the welfare of sentient beings in His creation would certainly be in keeping with a loving God.

In summary, I think the most we can say on the question of whether the God revealed by the book of nature is a person is that He is a person-like being who engaged, in the act of creation, in person-like activities.[2]

Before the creation, we might think of God as only the Ground of His own being, since there was no other being at that time, in the Planck Era. Then, in the act of creation, God became the Ground of Being for everything that emanated from Him. God's role, as the Ground of Being, implies other personal characteristics. He gives everything the power of being. He sustains everything in its beingness, in it being what it is.

We can add to these notions the fact that God can feel *personally present* to us. We will find illustrations of this fact in our next chapter, on mankind's experience of God. This fact, of course, does not prove God to be a person. But if God is the Ground of our Being, and if this God can feel personally present to us, it implies a personhood to God. Moreover, many

---

2. This is consistent with how God has been envisioned or imagined in much of theology. See, e.g., Robinson, *Honest to God*, 48–54, and Borg, *God We Never Knew*, ch. 3.

people feel they have a personal relationship with God, a person-to-person relationship, in other words.

Certainly a case can be made that God is only a fanciful invention of the human mind and that psychology can explain why this God feels personally present to some of us. Human beings, however, are part of nature. We evolved from the natural world. The elements that comprise our bodies are found in nature. These particles and forces are *of* God. They gave rise to our bodies, bodies with brains and minds, which are also part of nature. While the content of our minds is derived from our personal experience and the culture in which we live, the fact that we have minds stems from a biological organ that is part of nature. So, if our method is to turn to the book of nature for clues about God, we should include mankind as part of that book. And mankind, in all cultures and times, has consistently had the sense that the gods are persons. Not *human* persons, of course; they are divine persons. But still, they think, feel, act, and relate as persons do, as we humans experience and conceptualize such things.

To summarize, there are valid reasons to attribute a kind of personhood to God. As a purposeful creator, God has many implicit personal characteristics, and these are also revealed in the way many humans experience this God.

This personal God is in us as the ground of our being. We start with that. How then does He know and care about us?

How Does God Know About Us?

I want to get to the point of God caring about us, but for Him to care, He first has to know about us and the circumstances of our lives. How would God, as the Ground of our Being, know these things?

Let's go back to the beginning and ponder *how* God knew what He knew before the creation. I have maintained that He must have known His own nature and the laws of physics that would emanate from that nature, laws that would give rise to a certain kind of universe. He had to know that His purposes would not be a *fait accompli* because of random forces within His own nature, and yet He knew the odds favored the fulfillment of His purposes. But how did God know these things? What do we even mean by God "knowing" something?

It would be a mistake, I believe, to assume that God's knowledge is like our knowledge. We have lots of ways of knowing things, but we can never know for sure that we are grasping the real truth. Presumably, God's way of knowing would have to be immediate and certain in order for Him to base the creation on this knowledge. That is, I do not believe He would have proceeded with the creation if His knowledge of His own nature and the kind of universe that would evolve from it was only His best guess.

I think we need to assume (along with Plato and Einstein, for example) that there is such a thing as objective truth. Plato believed that something is true insofar as it *partakes* of the Form of the Truth (which is subsumed in the Form of the Good). His Divine Craftsman drew on this Form, which is the eternal essence of truth, in creating a world wherein things could be objectively true by virtue of this partaking. Plato does not say *how* the Divine Craftsman knew the truth, but a kind of direct, immediate access is implied. The God that we are speculating about must also have had a direct access to "the truth," at least as regards His own nature and the laws of physics that would grow from His nature and prevail in His universe.

My point is that God must have known the truth of things through a kind of direct, immediate, unambiguous apprehension. The theological doctrine of God's omniscience is built on this concept, although it incorrectly (in my view) extends God's knowledge to everything—past, present, and future. Surely, the God implied by the book of nature had to know some things, but not all things.

Because God is a person-like being who resides in us, as a foundational presence in every atom of our bodies, I believe it is reasonable to assume that he knows us, and knows the circumstances of our lives, through the same kind of direct, immediate apprehension of the truth. It would not be logical, in my view, to think that God knows about us through observation, since that is not how God knows things. We certainly know, from a human standpoint, how faulty observation can be when it comes to knowing the truth.

If God knows the truth about us, He knows us better than we know ourselves. He knows that we did not create ourselves and that we find ourselves being the person we are. We are a mystery to ourselves because we cannot possibly know all the causes that made us the way we are. But God knows these causes because they are part of our truth. If we search fearlessly into our innermost selves, who among us would not find some evil and ugliness there? God knows we did not *choose* to have these untoward tendencies or spiteful, resentful thoughts. We find ourselves having them, but God knows how and why they evolved in us, and does not judge or blame us. He has more compassion toward us than we could ever have ourselves, because God knows our truth and we do not.

Does God Personally Care About Us?

What about the proposition that God personally cares about us? I don't mean just that God cares about the fate of mankind; I mean that God cares about each one of us, perhaps in the manner that a parent cares about His children.

I imagine that most people who believe in a personal God *want* that God to care about them and indeed *believe* that He does. A common reason for wanting this God to care is that He will then be inclined to bestow blessings upon us or hold us in the safety of His hands. A caring God, in other words, would watch out for our well-being and intervene when our well-being was threatened. As I have said before, however, I do not see any logical reason to attribute to God the power to intervene in human affairs. I believe it is more logical to assume that God does *not* have such power, for if He were omnipotent, the vale of tears that afflicts mankind would not be so.

As an aside, I should mention here that it is not only the limits of God's power that keeps Him from intervening in our world; such intervention has also been considered unnecessary. In the Introduction I mentioned the Deistic movement that took hold among the intelligentsia of seventeenth-century Europe. The Deists believed that God created the best of all possible worlds, a world that ran like a finely tuned clock made by an infinitely skilled watchmaker, and that no divine intervention in the world was needed. They did not believe that miracles were possible or necessary. If the Deity did intervene to change things, it would mean the world was not so finely crafted after all, and this, the Deists could not fathom. The divine wisdom of the Deity was revealed in the perfect order of the world He created.

Getting back to whether God cares about us, I don't believe that our *wanting* God to care or *believing* He does makes any difference because God's caring is based on His love for us and His wisdom on what would be best for us. Nonetheless, I think there is a *logical basis* for believing in a caring God. It follows logically that God would care about the fulfillment of His purposes. If He created the world to propagate goodness, beauty, and love, He would not be indifferent to whether these purposes were actually realized as the universe unfolded. He would *care* about the realization of goodness, beauty, and love throughout His creation and for the sentient beings that evolved therein. And that would include us.

But Is a Caring God a Helpful God?

How can a caring God be of any help to us? The answer to that is not quite so straightforward. Let's consider this from God's point of view. He created the world with certain purposes in mind and the creation that emerged from His nature was instilled with the necessary means to maximize the fulfillment of those purposes. This power came from God. It is *of* God and reflects His nature. This is how God gave Himself over for the welfare of His creation.

The power of God is also within us, because God is the ground of our being. The aim of this power is to bring goodness, beauty, and love into our lives. That's what this power is for. When our well-being is threatened, we can tap into this power for the help we need. Sometimes we can change the situation we are in, but we need to draw on the power and inner resources that God has instilled in us. At other times, the negative situation is thrust upon us and our only constructive recourse is to make the best of the bad situation. Here again, God has instilled in us the necessary resources, *but we need to tap into them.*

A cynic might claim, in light of God's inability (in my view) to change the circumstances of our lives, that it doesn't matter if God cares about us or not because it does us no good. "Who cares if God cares about us," he might say, "He can't do anything to help us." My answer is that it matters to us in the most crucial of ways. Because He cares about the fulfillment of His purposes throughout the universe (*which includes us*), He has instilled in us the power and resources to change the circumstances of our lives, to the extent possible, and to hold ourselves steady against the misfortunes that befall us. If this were not the case, we would be ultimately alone in the unpredictable and perilous world in which we find ourselves. We all know how extremely vulnerable we are. There is so much that can go wrong in our bodies and minds. We can be profoundly hurt by the indifference or cruelty of others. The human condition is not a cakewalk for any of us. But God has imparted His spirit in the depth of our being, and with His spirit come the resources and power we need. This is the help God delivers.

When we look at our world, we find an abundance of evil, ugliness, and hate, as we all know. Many of us will admit to finding this in ourselves as well, in our hidden resentments and hostility, for example. As I've mentioned, I believe God knew the conflicting forces in His nature would give rise to a universe of mixed results—a universe primarily of goodness, beauty, and love, but also a universe where evil, ugliness, and hate could threaten His ultimate purposes. These mixed results are also present in us. Our human nature is a mixed bag. I don't believe God blames or judges us for the untoward tendencies in our nature. Nature itself is a mixed bag and can afflict us with all manner of suffering. I suspect our sorrow is God's sorrow, and that our longing for relief or rescue is God's wish He could do more.

When God let the creation fly loose in the big bang, He let Himself fly loose with it, becoming the Ground of Being for everything, everywhere.

As we've learned from Paul Tillich, the Ground of Being is also the *power* of being, the power within things to be what they are. And because this power is from God and *of* God, it carries with it the *intentionality of God*, which is the intention to maximize goodness, beauty, and love. God's purpose is everywhere and in everything. It is a purpose accompanied with the power to fulfill it. If we could peer into the innermost depth of every speck of matter and every spark of energy, we would find God's purposes hidden there, purposes that carry the power to fulfill them.

I want to underscore my main point here. Because God cares, He has ingrained His spirit in the core of our being, giving us the inner resources we need for the flourishing of goodness, beauty, and love within our life situation, and within ourselves. These inner resources are called many things: the human spirit, courage, hope, resolve, resilience, perspective, gratitude, compassion, acceptance, love of oneself, love of others (to name a few of the incarnations of God's power within us).

I wonder how this would apply to a person who was dying from a horrible illness (Lou Gehrig's Disease comes to mind). Such an illness would be an example of the evil and ugliness in God's world, a stark manifestation of the random chaos that can afflict us. Suppose while he was lying in bed, trying to prepare himself for the end that was coming, a sweet memory entered his mind, a remembrance of one joyful event from long ago that he had not thought about for many years. This one remembrance, perhaps held in safe keeping by the God within, would bring the smallest of consolations, but it would not be nothing. It would help to balance the scales ever so slightly. This might be the only help coming from the inner God, given the reality of the person's situation. But it would come from a God who cares and wishes He could do more.

On Caring About God

God's caring for us is not the same, of course, of our caring about Him. This is also something to consider. Do we care about His purposes? Do we feel personally devoted to helping His purposes prevail?

Normally we are too preoccupied with the demands of our own existence to be thinking about God. The welfare of our loved ones is often foremost on our minds. When we are ill, it is natural to be preoccupied with our physical state. There are countless reasons, in other words, for not even thinking about God's purposes. I believe our God is loving, compassionate, and understanding, and harbors no negative judgment about these matters. He certainly does not *need* us to care about Him. But still, He must want us to care about His purposes for our troubled world. And if we can help in some small way, through some act of kindness, we can imagine God is pleased.

In the Catholic religion, the Act of Contrition harbors a deep caring about God. "Oh my God I am heartily sorry for having offended thee . . ." Our sins supposedly offend God. The God of this book's theology is never offended because He is full of compassion toward anyone who sins. The sinner does not choose to be sinful. Bad things have happened to this person that caused him or her to disrespect the rights of others. The person was not born this way. God knows this, of course, and therefore never judges a person as being intentionally evil or cruel and is never personally offended by someone's behavior.

Why Pray to God?

As you know, I do not believe it makes sense to ask God to intervene in our lives, or in the lives of the people we love, or to ask for certain favors or blessings. I suppose that God, in His boundless caring for us, would do everything in His power to help us, at least with regard to bringing goodness, beauty, and love into our lives. But God (in my view) has no power whatsoever when it comes to changing what is going on in His creation. His power was to will the universe into being and to imbed Himself as the Ground of Being in all things. He knew full well that the laws of physics would take over and that the evolution of the universe would be mostly guided by deterministic laws that would support His purposes, but that random, chaotic forces would inevitably disrupt this process from time to time, in varying degrees.

Nonetheless, I believe it is wise to pray to our inner God because when we do this we are actually *calling forth* a power that resides in the deepest levels of our being. Early in this chapter, I discussed the many incarnations of God's power within us, a power that comes hand in hand with His caring for us. This power often comes forth on its own. I imagine that we constantly utilize, in one way or another, the resources that come from our divine core. We are not conscious of this, but we are continually making good and beautiful things happen for us and for each other.

There are times, however, when we need special or extraordinary help from within. Rather than passively hope for this help, we can actively solicit and implore it to come forth. This is what I believe prayer is for. God does not *intervene* to answer such prayers; He has already given us everything He possibly could. Now it is up to us to call on this power, to pray for it when we need it most.

As a clinical psychologist, I specialized in working with people who had cancer. One of my patients was terminally ill with metastatic breast cancer. She was only forty-two years old. The greatest joy in her life, she told me, was her ten-year old son, who had not yet reached his first birthday when she was diagnosed. She was not expected to survive more than a few years. And yet she had nine additional years to enjoy raising him and instilling in him everything of value that she found in herself. She was enormously grateful. She told me she could look ahead and feel cheated of all the years she would miss out on, or she could look back and feel grateful for every good thing in her life, and especially for being able to raise her son to age ten.

Then she learned, quite by accident, that new metastases meant that she probably had only three months to live. This news devastated her. "Three months!" she yelled in my office. "Only three fucking months!" She was so distraught and despondent that her gratitude, she told me, had flown right out the window. Then a brilliant thought came to her. She decided to pray for the return of her gratitude. She was not a deeply religious person; she had not been to church, she told me, or even prayed, for many, many years. So she was surprised when suddenly she had this thought, the thought of praying for the return of her gratitude. She said she prayed as she had never done before. It was not a prayer to God. She prayed to her lost gratitude, asking it to come back. And it did, just as strong and full as it had always been. Afterward, I wondered privately if the thought had come from God. But no, I do not believe God intervened to give her that thought. I believe it was a spontaneous manifestation of the God within her, the same God in each of us who is an ever-present resource for goodness, beauty, and love.

7

The Experience of God's Presence

IF WHAT I'VE SAID so far in this book is true, about the God who abides in the innermost aspect of who and what we are, then shouldn't we all experience the presence of this God on a daily basis? After all, if God is the Ground of our Being, and if this God is a person-like being who knows and cares about us, then why don't we actively experience His presence all the time?

Speaking personally, I yearn to feel His presence much more vividly and powerfully than I ever do. I am troubled and confused by this. I want our God to be personally present to me, but it often seems like there is no one there. At times I have really needed Him, for solace or strength or direction, but received nothing from Him, as far as I can tell. I have been left on my own to deal with whatever life throws at me.

Sometimes I have a vague sense of His presence within me, but to be truthful, I can't tell if it's just my imagination or wishful thinking. So I am thrown back to a basic existential quandary: the God I believe in seems so far away, so silent and indifferent. I have had to wonder: how is this God different from no God at all?

This question was posed years ago by the philosopher Anthony Flew.[1] He imagined two hikers, a believer and a skeptic, who come upon a clearing

---

1. Flew, *Introduction to Western Philosophy*.

in a dense forest. The believer claims that a gardener secretly tends to this clearing. The skeptic wants some proof and proposes that a video camera be set up to film this gardener. This is done and no gardener is filmed. The believer then says the gardener is invisible. The skeptic thinks this invisible gardener must have a scent that a dog could detect. A dog placed in the clearing and filmed for days, but never barks or shows any sign of detecting the gardener's scent. The believer simply claims the gardener has no scent. The skeptic then devises some sensors that would detect this invisible gardener. Still, the sensors detect nothing. The believer says the gardener is spiritual and cannot be detected by sensors. The skeptic then films the ground in the clearing for several days, claiming the dirt would show some disturbance if the clearing was being tended to. No movement of the dirt is found. The believer claims the tending of the clearing is done my magic, with no touching of the soil involved. In exasperation, the skeptic says: your gardener is invisible, scentless, spiritual, and works by magic. How is this gardener different from no gardener at all?

Of course I am not alone in wanting a more personal connection to God. It's a common human desire and a common lament throughout the ages. If we believe in any God at all, we certainly want Him to be real to us. A case can be made for a personal Creator Deity, as I've tried to show. *Why then does He seem so nonexistent?* That's our question.

I want to address this question in three ways. First, our God may seem unreachable because He actually *is* unreachable—that is, He is so deep within us that we can't reach to that depth, to the depth of our innermost being, as Saint Augustine put it (see below). That may be why we can't really touch Him, at least not consciously. That's the first issue I want to address.

The second issue is that each of us, I believe, experiences the movement or activity of the God within us when we have a welling up of a certain emotion, a sudden impulse to do something so good or loving that it seems out of character, or a sudden insight into a problem or dilemma that confronts us. We can ask ourselves, "Where did that come from?" We do not recognize it as coming from God, even though the theology presented in this book suggests that such manifestations of our humanness come from a divine source within us.

The third answer is that many of our fellow humans genuinely seem to experience the personal presence of God and recognize this presence or visitation as coming from God. Their experience of this presence could suggest that God is not so unreachable after all. In his classic study *The Varieties of Religious Experience*, William James reviews the personal testimonials of countless people who have, they believe, encountered God's presence within them.

In his analysis of these testimonials, Professor James is not afraid to explore two main possibilities: Do they point to something that is true about the God of religion? Or do they reveal a particular sort of psychiatric disturbance, such as a delusionary or hallucinogenic sense of a visitation by a spiritual being? We will turn to his analysis to see if it helps answer the question we are grappling with, namely, are there any aspects of our experience that point to the God within?

Is God Beyond Our Reach?

In the history of theology, God has been conceptualized as so transcendent, so much above and beyond anything that we can experience, that He is simply beyond our reach. He has also been conceptualized being so deeply imbedded in the fabric of all reality, and so deeply within the fabric of our being, that He is beyond our reach for that reason. We cannot reach to the height of God or penetrate to the depth of God.

Also in the history of theology, we find the notion that God is not so transcendent or so deep that He cannot touch us. But this is always God's doing. Tillich was fond of saying we are often grasped by the Ground of our Being or by our Ultimate Concern, which he believed was another way of conceptualizing the *manifestation* of the God within. If these ideas are correct, that we can be touched by God, then the question arises: Why aren't we, or why don't we know it?

The God unveiled in what we've learned from modern physics is found in the fundamental, foundational particles and forces that makeup our world. These particles and forces are not literally God, as I have said many times; rather, they are *of God*, in that God is their ultimate source, that God sustains them in being what they are, and that God's nature and purposes are revealed through them. God is radically deep in every speck of matter and in every spark of energy. That means God is radically deep in us too. Is He so radically deep to be beyond our reach?

Saint Augustine would answer "yes" to that question. He once remarked that God was "more inside me than my inmost part"[2] (in this footnote I offer some other translations of the relevant Latin text). This passage has received a good deal of theological attention as scholars have sought to discern Augustine's meaning. Perhaps he was referring to his basic sense of

---

2. Augustine, *Confessions*, bk. 3, ch. 6, para. 1. The relevant quotation, in Latin, reads *Deus interior intimo meo*, which has been variously translated as "God is more intimate to me than I am to myself," "God is more inside me than my inmost part," and "God is nearer to me than I am to myself."

self as his "inmost part." Most essentially, most fundamentally, and most deeply, he was a self. And yet his inner God was deeper still, dwelling in a depth we cannot reach.

Augustine felt close to himself, but he felt God was closer still. I don't think he meant that God was in closer *proximity* to himself. Rather, I think he was referring to the closeness of two entities, where one had virtually merged with they other. God had merged into him; that's how radically close they were. He did not share that same kind of closeness with his sense of self.

This is Augustine's answer to our question. God is not unreachable because He is too transcendent, too far above and beyond us. Nor is He too "other" or beyond what we can conceptualize. The problem concerns His radical immanence. He is *one with us*, and thus too close and merged with the depth of our being. We cannot step back and experience our closeness to Him because there is no stepping back from God.

Can God Reach Us?

The second way I want to approach the question of this chapter—namely, why does a supposedly immanent God seem so remote or nonexistent—is by considering those experiences wherein we find ourselves suddenly feeling something profound, suddenly grasping a key insight, or suddenly doing something unexpected that was astonishingly right. Where did that come from? Haven't we all asked ourselves this question from time to time? We might sense that something profound moved within us—a startling emotion, a penetrating insight, a stunningly correct action.

Here is a real-life example that I know well when I worked with cancer patients before working on this book. I ran a support group for husbands whose wives had cancer. A member of this group, a man in his mid-thirties, was facing the loss of his wife, who was terminally ill. She was bravely realistic about her situation, and often sobbed, he told us, about having to die while still so young. He suddenly had an idea that he knew would help her find some peace as her death approached.

He wrote to as many of her friends and relatives he could think of (and find addresses for) and asked if they would write some special memories about her and send any photos of her that they thought had special significance. His idea, he explained to these relatives and friends, was to create a binder for her as a testimonial to how loved and special she was. He explained to the group that she had touched many people and he felt this binder would be a tribute to this fact, and underscore one aspect of her life's meaning. She once lamented, he told us, that her life had been too short to amount to anything important or lasting. He hoped this binder would help offset this feeling.

Cards and letters and photos came pouring in, and he began arranging these in a tastefully-decorated binder. As her illness progressed she was spending more and more time in bed, and wished their bedroom could be painted a more soothing color than the standard off-white. He said he'd be happy to repaint it and brought home a number of color samples he thought she'd like. If I recall correctly, I believe she chose a soft sage green color. She apparently loved the new color and found the bedroom a more comforting place to be. He found some color paper that matched the walls, and used that paper to make the pages for the binder. He then glued the cards and photos from her loved ones on these pages.

When he gave her this binder, at first she didn't know what it contained. But then she started to page through it and the tears began to flow. He said she was literally speechless when she tried to thank him. He said she kept it in bed with her until the day she died.

In one of our group meetings I asked him how he got this idea, the idea of making this binder for her. Had he ever heard of such a thing being done, I wondered. He said no, that the idea just came to him. "It came from where?" I recall asking. He could not say; it just came, it was just there.

An additional aspect of this idea was that it was *for her*, as opposed to an idea that would help him. He was not thinking about his own needs. He was not wondering how he was going to deal with losing his wife or how he was going to go on with his own life in a positive way. He was thinking of helping *her* deal with *her* death. Certainly it helped him in knowing that he did it and in seeing the overwhelmingly powerful and positive effect it had. But this was not his motivation.

I want to offer a theological answer to the question I posed to him, about the *source* of this idea. It is an answer that draws on the theology of this book. In chapter 3 I took up the question of God's purposes and speculated that they concerned the propagation of goodness, beauty, and love. These purposes created a *push* in all creation, a push or drive toward goodness, beauty, and love. This push was and is inherent in God's nature. And because we are *of God*, His purposes are alive within us, and so is the push I mentioned. In the example I've given, the husband's idea and actions can be seen in this light. They sprang forth from the divine core within him. That was their source.

I offered this one example to illustrate a question and a theological answer to it. How many other examples are there of this same phenomenon, this same push, in human history? Certainly too many to count. We'd have to figure the number of humans that existed, and for each of them, the millions of ideas that came into their minds, and all of their resulting actions. Not all of these ideas and actions can be interpreted as coming from God, embodying the same divine push. But certainly a countless number can be understood from that perspective.

It is fair to ask, if what I have said is correct, why there are so many ideas, and so many actions, that run counter to the push I've described. If God is embodied in the fabric of being, why don't we find *more* goodness, beauty, and love in human history? Why is there so much of the opposite, of so much evil, ugliness, and hatred? I will take up this vexing issue in chapter 8.

Has God, In Fact, Come to Many of Us?

The third answer to the question we are exploring, as I mentioned earlier, is that many of our fellow humans have genuinely experienced, they believe, the personal presence of God within them or have sensed the presence of God in the world at large. What are we to make of their experiences, which they have described in powerful, personal testimonials? Do these show that the God of religion is real, or do they prove that people can delude themselves into believing all sorts of things? That was the question William James took up in his classic study *The Varieties of Religious Experience*. At the time, James was a professor of philosophy and psychology at Harvard University.

In this book, Professor James examines the testimonials of numerous people (in centuries past, up to the present) who have experienced God in a personal and profoundly impactful way. This, in any event, is what they genuinely believe. In his analysis of these testimonials, James is, first of all, consistently respectful toward the believers who have recorded their experience of God's presence in the world and within themselves, and secondly, he is consistently interested in what they mean. The question of the meaning of these testimonials has two aspects. One concerns the meaning of the experience of God to those who have had these experiences. The other concerns their meaning to the larger question of God's existence, the God of religion, that is. This was James's main interest.

Pages 38–233 of James's work,[3] delivered in 1901–1902 as the Gifford Lectures at the University of Edinburgh in Scotland, is replete with written or recorded testimonials of religious experience. First, James outlines the types or varieties of these experiences, and then quotes from those who have had such experiences, including saints, mystics, clergymen, various

---

3. James, *Varieties of Religious Experience*.

lay spiritual seekers, as well as individuals who had not thought of themselves as religious or spiritual until a transformative experience of the divine changed their beliefs and orientation toward the world. These lectures and testimonials set the stage for his remarkable concluding lecture in which he captures the common aspects of these experiences and then tackles the question of what they mean.

Because our current chapter focuses on the personal experience of an inner God, I will offer a few brief examples of the testimonials presented in James's work that concern this particular type of religious experience.

The clergyman James Russell Lowell wrote of a "revelation" that came to him while he was debating certain spiritual matters with a colleague:

> While I was speaking, something rose up before me like a vague destiny looming from the Abyss. I never before felt so clearly the spirit of God in me and around me. The whole room seemed to me full of God. The air seemed to waiver to and fro with the presence of Something I knew not what. I spoke with the calmness and clearness of a prophet. I cannot tell you what this revelation was. I have not yet studied it enough. But I shall perfect it one day and then you shall hear of it and acknowledge its grandeur.[4]

Another clergyman wrote of a similar experience in a more fully developed way:

> I remember the night, and almost the very spot on the hill-top, where my soul opened out, as it were, into the Infinite, and there was a rushing together of the two worlds, the inner and outer. . . . I stood alone with Him who made me, and all the beauty of the world, and love and sorrow, enveloped together. I did not seek Him, but felt the perfect unison of my spirit with His. The ordinary sense of things around me faded. For the moment nothing but an ineffable joy and exultation remained. It is impossible to fully describe the experience. It was like the effect of some great orchestra when all the separate notes have melted into one swelling harmony that leave the listener conscious of nothing save that his soul is being wafted upwards, and almost bursting with its own emotion. The perfect stillness of the night was thrilled by a more solemn silence. The darkness held a presence because it was all the more felt because it was not seen. I could not anymore doubt that He was there than I was. Indeed, I felt myself to be, if possible, the less real of the two. My highest

---

4. James, *Varieties of Religious Experience*, 43.

faith in God and truest idea of Him were then born in me....
I believe I stood face to face with God, and was born anew of
His spirit.... Having once felt the presence of this spirit, I have
never lost it again.[5]

A final example comes from a testimonial that James translated from the original French. The writer describes a hike wherein he felt in perfect health, full of energy and positive emotion, with no stress or uncertainty about the path they were on.

> When all at once I experienced a feeling of being raised above myself. I felt the presence of God, as if His goodness and power were penetrating me altogether. The throb of emotion was so violent that I could barely tell the boys to pass on and not wait for me. I then sat down on a stone, unable to stand any longer, and my eyes overflowed with tears. I thanked God that in the course of my life He had taught me to know Him, that He sustained my life.... The impression was so strong I asked myself if it were possible that Moses on Sinai could have had a more intimate communion with God. I think it well to add that in this ecstasy of mine God had neither form, color, odor, nor taste; moreover, that the feeling of His presence was accompanied with not determinate localization. It was rather as if my personality had been transformed by the presence of a spiritual spirit. ... God was present, though invisible; He fell under not one of my senses, yet my consciousness perceived Him.[6]

Examples such as these go on and on in James's text. For me, they became tiresome. I had the impression that he wanted to show he was not afraid of facing the sheering testimony of so many believers. After a few hundred pages of such testimony, he could never be accused of glossing over this aspect of the human experience. Rather, it gives the impression that he *must* come to terms with it. That we all must. I believe this was his real purpose.

Before he takes up this challenge, he summarizes the key aspects that he has gleaned from the testimonials, the key aspects of religious experience, in other words ... aspects that apply across the board. He identifies the following:[7]

---

5. James, *Varieties of Religious Experience*, 44–45.
6. James, *Varieties of Religious Experience*, 45.
7. These are presented in James, *Varieties of Religious Experience*, 271–83.

1. The testimonials emphasize the primacy of feeling over intellectual content. Feeling the divine presence evokes changes in behavior, but does not generally evoke more abstract thoughts or theories.

2. The feelings that arise, when encountering God's presence, are generally ones of rapture, cheerfulness, expansiveness, and readiness for great things. James cites Tolstoy's point that faith is a force by which men live. This force, James notes, is alive in the hearts of those who have encountered God; these believers are less concerned with the truth-claims of their experience.

3. Religious experience helps believers to carry out their spiritual purposes—which are essential and vital to what matters most to them—over-against the pressures of the world to seek worldly gratification only. The "larger power" in the world is "friendly" to ourselves and our ideals.

4. Religious experience commonly derives from a sense that there is something wrong with us as we naturally are, and that we therefore need to be saved from this wrongness by making connection with the higher powers at work in God's creation. Believers often feel, James asserts, that a higher part of the self comes forth in their experience of God.

5. In keeping with the above, another common belief is that there is something *more* in the universe than meets the eye or that science can discern, and that this something more gives rise to the more (or higher part) within us that comes forth in God's presence. The world, when seen religiously, is not just a materialistic world. There is a deeper ideal level within it. This notion of something more is the common aspect of religious experience; sometimes, however, it is called the God within us that brings about our salvation.

6. The something more that grounds religious experience is, first of all, a personal God, but it is also a stream of ideal tendency or ideal order embedded in the structure of the world. There is a tendency or push in the world to bring about God's nature and purposes, and this actually causes good things to happen, independent from our belief or participation. But when we abandon ourselves to this tendency, it causes us to do good things and brings about our salvation. The reality of this something more is seen in its effects. It is real in that sense.

7. The ideal order that grounds religious experience is guaranteed by God's existence and is permanently preserved because of it.

8. Religious experience commonly testifies to the "invasions" of a deeper region within ourselves and our world.

9. A common belief is that God is present to all beings in the universe, who are therefore secure in His parental hands. We are all saved.

James believes that if there truly is a God, then there must be real differences in the way the world works as compared to a world where there is no God. These real differences are testified to in religious experience. If there are no real differences, then James would wonder how the God of religion is different from no God at all.

James notes that religious experience points to certain "facts" about the world. These various facts are seen in items 1–9 above. James wants to know, *Are these facts true?*

His first answer to this question is simply that it is impossible to know.[8] But he also takes up the question of what it means for something to be true. "The propensity of man," he writes, "is to believe that whatever has great value for life is thereby certified as true."[9] On this score, one could say that the belief in God is true. He cites numerous examples of the positive effects of this belief in the lives of those who believe they have encountered the God within. This belief, however, could be a delusion or hallucination, and still have positive effects. It could be argued, however, that these effects are not truly positive if they are based on a psychiatric syndrome. Suppose a person believes that God has visited them personally and called them to feed the hungry. Would it be positive for the person to heed this call even if the God who gives it does not really exist?

James also tackles the question of the "something more" that is common in religious experience. Does this really exist, he asks.

The emergence of a deeper part of ourselves, a something more, is a common aspect of religious experience. James notes that this deeper part is called the subconscious self in psychiatric science and that this deeper self within us can produce real and positive effects. In that sense, there is something more within us that we are not aware of, a something more that truly exists. James notes that a religious person can feel moved by an inner force and attribute it to the God within, whereas it can be explained scientifically as the emergence or activity of the subconscious self.

James, however, does not want to say, "See. It all can be explained scientifically. There is nothing more to religious experience than the stirrings

---

8. James, *Varieties of Religious Experience*, 264.
9. James, *Varieties of Religious Experience*, 275.

of the subconscious or the activity of a delusional or deranged mind." This is not *his* conclusion, although he grants that this conclusion may be valid.

At the conclusion of his book, James returns to the question he posed earlier: Are the facts about the world—the facts that religious experience points to, the facts that he summarized in items 1–9 above—*are these facts true?* James believes the answer is yes, that these facts are essentially true. He does not believe they are true in all their details, but their essence is correct. The scientific view is that they are not true. Most basically, the God posited by these "facts" does not exist. The belief in His existence can be explained by psychiatric science, which has been proven to be true. But this science, James believes, is far too narrow to capture the breath and complexity of human experience, and there is no science that can *disprove* God's existence and activity in the world.

A key conclusion reads as follows: "The total expression of human experience, as I view it objectively, invincibly urges me beyond the narrow 'scientific' bounds. Assuredly, the real world is of a different temperament—more intricately built than physical science allows."[10]

---

10. James, *Varieties of Religious Experience*, 280.

8

God and the Problem of Evil

WHERE IS GOD IN the suffering and evil that happen to everyone, at least from time to time? If God is all-powerful and all-loving, why does He allow this to occur? And if God is perfect in his justice, why does He allow the perfectly innocent to suffer horribly? This is the problem of evil in a nutshell, perhaps the strongest nail in God's coffin.[1,2,3] For many people, over many centuries, it proves that the God of religion is dead or never existed. This God—the one disproved by the problem of evil—is supposedly bursting with love for all His creation and holds the power to make things right. He is thought to be a perfect being and thus perfect in all His attributes. Starting with this premise, it is assumed that God is perfectly good, perfectly loving, perfectly just, and perfect in knowledge and power. His perfection is also infinite. Thus, He is infinitely good, loving, just, knowledgeable, and powerful. How could such a God cause or allow innocent suffering? It defies all logic and proves that this (fairy tale) God must not exist.

Let's consider a child who is dying of cancer, and let's consider what the God described above would do about it, given the infinite perfection

---

1. See, e.g., Tooley, "Problem of Evil."
2. Altizer and Hamilton, *Radical Theology*, 23–52.
3. Padovano, *Estranged God*, 101–37.

of His many attributes. First, God would know about this child's suffering because His knowledge is perfect. God knows everything. Next, God would love this child because His love knows no limits. Because this child is innocent, God in His perfect justice would intervene to save her. And of course God would have the power to do this, because of His omnipotence. The fact that this child suffers and dies is an insurmountable and heartbreaking problem for belief in God. It either exposes the weakness and/or callousness of God, or it exposes the fallacy of His very existence. That's the problem of evil, a problem that theists detest and a problem that atheists love, for it proves them right in rejecting the existence of God.

The problem of evil is not just a theological quandary. It goes far beyond that. For every theologian who has tried to figure out a logical solution, there are a multitude of non-theologians who have been driven to despair, bitterness, and the loss of their faith because their God appears to be so remote, uncaring, and powerless. Every believer is in this same boat, call it the boat of heartbreak and anguish, for every believer suffers and the God of their belief never clearly intervenes to end their suffering. And every believer has people in their life they love dearly, and they suffer too, causing every believer to pray in their own way for God's mercy. If I believed in the God of religion, and if one of my children became terminally ill and died, I would want to storm the church I attended in my youth, dose the pews and alter with gasoline, and sob inconsolably as I watched it burn. My point is that the problem of evil is also an emotional quandary. The emotions it causes can ruin a person's faith.

The God of my faith, thankfully, would sob at my side, having loved my child and loved me. And He'd be weeping for Himself as well, for His inability to prevent such a thing.

As you know from previous chapters, the problem of evil is *not* a basis for rejecting the God of this book's theology. I argued in chapter 4 that this God lacked the power to make a perfect world, and lacked the power to do everything that His compassion and love would want Him to do. Instead of making us turn away from Him, the problem of evil can cause us to turn toward God, toward the ground of our being that is a wellspring of resilience, fortitude, and perspective.

In what follows, I want to summarize those aspects of this book's theology that have a direct bearing on the problem of evil. The most relevant aspects concern the question of God's power and the havoc wrought by the randomness inherent in God's nature.

On God, Power, and Evil

Chapter 2 offered a story about God the creator and the possible purposes of His creation. God willed the universe into being, and his willing it caused that to happen. The creation therefore revealed God's power, the power that came from His will. The universe that emanated or flowed from his nature is made up of certain fundamental building blocks and forces, and these are manifestations of God's nature. What do these building blocks and forces reveal about God? That's a key question in this book, and for all of theology, in my view.

The God of this book's theology, with His will and power, launched the universe and got things started, but He is not an active agent with the power to intervene to change what is occurring. God's power was the power to set the universe in motion. *What happens in the universe is the result of causal laws and random forces that were put there in the beginning.* This is what the created world reveals. It reveals laws and forces that account for what happens; it does not reveal an active agent who intervenes to change things.

While the laws of causality are an essential aspect of our universe, they do not reign supreme. There are also random forces at work that can disrupt the workings of these laws. I introduced the reality of randomness in chapter 1. Modern physics reveals that some things in nature "just happen" outside the causal laws that normally prevail. They are not the consequence of known causes. Einstein believed that unknown causes were actually at work in what appears to be random, but that they were too deeply hidden to be discernible. But as we learned, quantum mechanics has shown that some occurrences are truly random; they are *not* caused in a deterministic fashion by forces or events that preceded them. This understanding of randomness is central to the occurrence of events we consider to be evil.

This evil is all too apparent on our own planet, where the havoc wrought by the chaotic randomness that impedes God's purposes is present everywhere. Think of all the deadly and crippling diseases we are vulnerable to. Think of all the children born retarded or with horrible bodily defects. Think of the viruses and infections that can overwhelm our immune system. Think of all the mental illnesses we are subject to, and think of the disintegration of our brains and minds that afflict so many of us in old age. These examples barely scratch the surface of the suffering that comes from being human. We suffer this way because of the disruption of orderly processes caused by random mutations, random infections, or the random disintegration that affects some minds. Our bodies and minds are vulnerable to random chaos in our cells. Of course, if a tally could be done of all the randomly-caused suffering in our world, alongside a tally of all the love, health, and happiness in our world, perhaps the verdict would be in our favor, that overall, God's purposes are thriving here.

The laws of causality that exist in the world imply that principles of causality were embedded in God's nature. I am saying this to be consistent with the point that our universe, in its fundamental makeup, emanated from God, and causality is certainly a fundamental aspect of our world.

The same can be said of the random forces we find in our world; these also came from God and mirror an intrinsic aspect of His nature. These forces were a given within God; He did not choose or cause them to be what they are. And yet the evil in our world show what can happen when randomness gets the upper hand. If God's purposes reigned supreme, there would only be good, beautiful, and loving events in His creation; as things stand, however, randomness can break or disrupt the causal chain that would otherwise guarantee the fulfillment of His purposes.

As an aside, in the prayer attributed to Jesus, he taught his followers to pray for God's will to be done on earth as it is in heaven. God's will is not automatically done in our world; it is something to be prayed for. My understanding of this, based on the theology in this book, is that God's will is not automatically done because of the random forces that can prevent it.

The randomness that particle physics has found in the workings of nature can lead to chaos and disorder and, by extension, to the "evil" in our world (I am putting "evil" in quotation marks because I recast the meaning of this term in the next section). In chapter 2, I maintained that God was not responsible for this evil. The randomness at work resulted from His nature, and yet God did not create His own nature.

As I've mentioned before, God is not to be blamed for evil because He lacked the power to create a perfect world or the power to intervene to prevent evil. He lacked this power because He could only create a world that was allowed by His nature, a world that was mostly good but sometimes corrupted by randomness.

What is the Essence of Evil and How did It Come About?

I think there are two key questions we need to confront at this juncture. First, what do we mean by "evil"? When we say something is evil, is that because it seems evil to us, perhaps due to our biased perspective? Or is it a correct conclusion because certain events and occurrences are truly evil, embodying the essential and intrinsic nature of evil? But if this were true, it would be a vexing theological problem. How can there be true evil in

God's world if this world emanated from God Himself and if there is no evil in God?

These are central questions for the theology of this book, and for all theology, in my view. Depending on how it's conceptualized, the existence of evil can ruin an otherwise sound theology. For example, I maintained in chapter 1 that all of creation flowed from God's nature; thus, the evil in the world, if we grant that its *essence* was embedded in the created world, would suggest that evil was embedded in God's nature. *It is the task of theology, in my view, to find an explanation about evil that does not undermine the God of love.* This is the challenge I am taking up in this section.

The Old Testament has an answer to the question of how evil originated and became a threat to the fulfillment of God's purposes. In the books of Isaiah and Ezekiel, the forces of evil that are pitted against God's will originated in the power of Lucifer, a fallen angel.

The theology I am developing in this book offers a different conceptualization of evil and how it came to be in God's universe. In what follows, I will be making the case that while many events and circumstances are understandably considered to be evil, they actually lack any inherent evilness. Let me explain.

I need to borrow a concept from philosophy (especially the philosophy of Plato) pertaining to the *ontological* status of something, for this is what, in my view, evil lacks. It has no ontological status. There is no such thing as inherent evilness. In philosophy, ontology refers to the innermost being or essence of something. When we ask, what is it that makes something what it is, we are asking an ontological question. We are asking about its essence. And if something has an inherent and enduring essence, it has ontological status.

If something seems to be real, but isn't really, it has no ontological status. A mirage, for example, is not ontologically real.

In Plato's philosophy, goodness and beauty have an inherent ontology in what he calls their ideal form. This is their eternal, enduring essence. Plato's ideal forms exists in an abstract realm where the pure essence of things lives. Even if there were nothing good or beautiful in the real world, goodness and beauty would still exist in this ideal realm. And if something in the real world is *truly* good or beautiful, it is only because the ideal form of goodness or beauty is manifested in it.

In philosophy generally, there is a distinction between something's existential reality and underlying essence or ontological being. The former refers to the way something exists in our world, in the world of appearance, the world we perceive. A painting, for example, can look beautiful to us. It is existentially beautiful because we find beauty in the way it exists. This does not necessarily mean the painting is ontologically beautiful. It could lack the essence of beauty in its innermost being. We might say, for example, that it *looks* beautiful but is not *really* beautiful. Following Plato, we would say it did not embody the ideal form or pure essence of beauty.

How do these concepts apply to the problem of evil? The evil that we encounter in ourselves and in our world is existentially real but lacks ontological status. The evil of war and disease are evil to us, they are part of our human existence, and threaten that existence; thus, they are *existentially* real. But they are not ontologically real because they do not manifest an ideal form or inherent essence of evil. *This is because, in the theology of this book, there is no ideal form of evil in God's world.* Again, Plato would say there is an ideal form of Goodness and Beauty, but not of Evil.

If the evil that we encounter is not ontologically real, is *not* a manifestation of an ideal form of Evil, and does *not* embody an enduring and eternal essence of evil, what then is it? What is it a manifestation of? How did it get into our world . . . into God's world?

This is where we see the havoc wrought by the random forces in the universe. Were it not for these forces, the Goodness, Beauty, and Love in God's nature (see ch. 3) would prevail in the causal chain that gave rise to us and the world in which we find ourselves. Randomness disrupts the causal chain and allows for outcomes that are not good, beautiful, or loving.

The child I mentioned at the beginning, who was dying if cancer, is an illustration of this. Cancer is the result of genetic mutations that have no known cause, and are thus considered to be random. This kind of thing can, and does, happen in God's creation. That's because there are random forces at work, forces that can cause havoc in the normal, lawful process of cell division. Usually when cells divide the daughter cells are exact copies of the mother cell. A daughter cell can only become malignant if some unknown force (call it random) causes a reordering of the molecules that make up the cell's DNA. When the malignant cell divides, it passes on its disordered DNA. These malignant cells can be further deranged by random forces, creating a slightly different malignant clone. Because of this, a medical intervention designed to target the initial malignant clone will not work against the subsequent clones. Oncologists often refer to cancer as a moving target. It dashes about because of random forces.

I can imagine a dialogue with God, a dialogue wherein we challenged Him by asking why He created a universe where things like this could happen. God would answer that cancer is the exception to the rule. Usually cells divide in a lawful, orderly way, without interference by random forces. He might remind us that the universe is mostly good and beautiful, and steeped in the love that flows from His nature. On balance, His purposes are prevailing. But still, sometimes random forces get the upper hand and things like cancer and horrifying birth defects can result. He would convey His profound sorrow about that. He would wish that His nature was *only* lawful and orderly, without the randomness that can cause evil and suffering.

A child with cancer is just one example of what random forces can do. They also account for a host of natural disasters that would never exist if the natural laws on our planet reflected the better angles of God, uncorrupted by randomness. These outcomes are *not* defined by the evil they supposedly embody, but rather by what they lack. And what they lack is the goodness, beauty, and love that God wants but can't make happen. He can't will randomness away. It is part of His nature. He is stuck with it and so are we. This is what we call "evil." This is what evil essentially *is*.

How Can God Help?

According to the theology being developed here, God cannot and does not *intervene* to rescue us from our suffering. He does not instill in us a kind of grace that makes us immune to suffering, a grace, for example, that would enable a saint to smile as she was being burned at the stake. Nor does He intervene to negate the cause of our suffering; He doesn't cure our diseases, stop earthquakes, put out fires, or diffuse bombs so they don't explode, to name a few examples. Therefore, we must ask: How can God help us? This book's theology, and any theology, must be pressed on this issue.

In chapter 6 I explored the concept of a personal God and the sense in which this God resides within us as a powerful resource. I said it would be an anthropomorphic error to assert that God was a person, as that would be a projection of a human concept onto God. Nonetheless, I argued that it was reasonable to attribute a kind of personhood to God, and that our relationship to God can certainly feel personal. The theology of this book also provides a basis for believing that God knows and cares about us and, what's more, as the ground of our being, helps us hold steady against the slings and arrows of our misfortune.

I want to say more here about God and our suffering. The notion that God suffers with us is an arresting theological concept,[4] and it was the theologian and Nazi resister Dietrich Bonhoeffer who (to the best of my knowledge) underscored the point that God's suffering was actually necessary as a precondition for His helping us in our own suffering.[5] Bonhoeffer believed

---

4. For review, see Bauchham, *Only a Suffering God Can Help*, 6–12.
5. Bonhoeffer, *Letters and Papers from Prison*, 348–70.

that God could empathize with our suffering because He suffered too. The question before us, however, concerns the manner in which God (whether He suffers or not) can and does help us.

Paul Tillich also grappled with this question. In *The Courage to Be*,[6] he wrote about the many ways in which we suffer, and was immeasurably impressed that so many of us are able to hold on to our faith, and to affirm the goodness of life, *in spite of* our suffering. He was thinking of people who do not deny or downplay their suffering. Nor do they seek to rise above it, saying to themselves: It's not so bad; It could be worse; or, Other people have suffered more. No, he was thinking of people who suffered fully and miserably, and yet, *in spite of it*, were able to love God and to love life. His question was: How were they able to do that? Where did their inner resolve come from? What was its source? His answer was not psychological. It was theological. The source was the God within them, the Ground of their being.

In this book, we are embarked on a psychological, philosophical, and theological quest. Because we are part of nature, we want to explore what the God of nature means for us. Specifically, what does it mean to say we are *of God*? I first introduced this way of thinking about our existence in chapter 1 and have come back to it many times. We are *of God* in the sense that we came from God, just as everything in the natural world did. But we are also *of God* in the sense that our innermost being pulsates with God's will and purposes. Paul Tillich called this the Ground of our Being; Abraham Lincoln referred to it as "the better angels of our nature" in his first inaugural address.

I also like the metaphor that God is like a seed within us. A seed is packed with the potential to grow, but it will not grow if it is left alone. It must be nurtured by soil, water, and energy from the sun. The seed's potential will then be unlocked. When a seed grows, it doesn't just become a larger seed. It becomes what the seed stipulates or calls forth.

This metaphor points to the role we can play in calling forth the God within us or in tapping into the potential that this God encapsulates. As I said in chapter 6, this is one way of thinking about a prayer to God. This would not be a prayer for God to intervene to change the circumstances of our lives, the lives of our loved ones, the welfare of humanity as a whole, or the welfare of our planet. As you know, this book's theology does not provide a basis for an interventionist God. But calling forth the God within us, whether in prayer or a simple thought, when we feel in need of fortitude, endurance, or inspiration, is not asking for God to intervene. It is asking

---

6. Tillich, *Courage to Be*.

for our inner God and the goodness, beauty, and love embodied in Him to come forth, to grow and flourish.

One problem with the seed metaphor, however, is that it implies that the God within us lies dormant if He is not nurtured in some way. I believe the potential within us, the potential that is *of God*, can influence us without being nurtured or called forth. In the movie *Schindler's List*, the protagonist who saved the Jewish workers under him probably had no awareness of being moved by God, and yet he most certainly was (in the theology of this book).

The problem of evil is not a problem for believing in the God of this book. It is, however, a problem *for* this God. In chapter 2, I speculated about God's purposes as He willed the universe into being. As I've mentioned many time, He did that to promulgate the goodness, beauty, and love that were intrinsic to His nature. The evil in our world can viciously undermine these purposes. That's the true problem of evil.

God helps us by being who He is for us. He is our source and our wellspring for holding steady against the slings and arrows of our misfortune, as I said before. Holding steady means that God's purposes prevail in us *in spite of* the suffering that evil brings. We can hold on to the goodness, beauty, and love in our nature because we are *of God*. God's purposes are alive within us. They give us power, the power to prevail over evil, ugliness, and hate when beset with evil.

This is who God is for us. This is how He helps.

As you know, I speculated about God's purposes as related to goodness, beauty, and love in chapter 2. Perhaps that was a stretch on my part, for how can we really know about these specific purposes? But in chapter 1 I offered a more general way of thinking about God's purpose. It was based on the simple idea that God was good and that He willed His creation to be good. This conception of God's purpose was meant to be the most basic or elementary. The fulfillment of this purpose, however, was not a sure thing. It was threatened by random forces, and this threat persists to the present time. God was taking a chance, therefore, in setting the universe in motion.

The evil and suffering that randomness can bring into the world, and into our lives, *could* prevail over goodness. But God must have believed that goodness would prevail, and on that basis, He let His creation fly free.

A question for us, therefore, is how we might promote God's cause or God's purpose over the course of our lives. We can do that by embracing and enhancing goodness whenever we can, even especially when we are confronted with evil and suffering. It's a cliché to say we should always strive to make the best of a bad situation. And yet this is exactly what the God within us can help us to do. We find a searing example of this in the late

Viktor Frankl, the esteemed Austrian psychiatrist and holocaust survivor. In *Man's Search for Meaning*, he described the horrific suffering that he and his fellow inmates endured in a Nazi concentration camp. And yet rather than allow this suffering to deaden their will to live or create bitterness and despair, they turned their suffering into a personal triumph by prevailing over it—not by suffering less, but by maintaining hope, tenacity, and their love of life in spite of their suffering. This was their personal triumph. This was how they found meaning in their suffering. This was how, in the theology of this book, they held tight to the push toward goodness because they were *of God* in the core of their being. And this was how they contributed to God's cause.

That deep part of us that is *of God* constantly calls to us. Sometimes called our soul, it does not sit quietly or passively within us. The ground of our being is a rich and fertile soil. It is bursting with God's will. It is bursting with the power that God has instilled in all of His creation. That power is in us too, the power to bring forth goodness, beauty, and love wherever and however we can. Perhaps most especially when we are suffering, this power from God is there to help us endure.

The call in us that is *of God*, and the power it imparts, was echoed in the words attributed to Jesus in Matthew's gospel: *Come unto me, all ye that labor and are heavy laden, and I will give you rest. Shoulder my yoke and learn from me, for I am gentle and humble of heart, and you will find rest for your souls* (Matt 11:28–30).[7]

---

7. I am not citing this passage because I believe it's the word of God. Rather, the sentiment it expresses was ingrained in the Jewish culture and tradition, and was embraced by the early followers of Jesus, and thus found its way into Matthew's gospel.

9

A Theology of Death

DEATH IS WOVEN INTO the fabric of God's world, and we have to wonder why. At least in the world we live in, all life ends in death. This could be the case wherever life might be, but we only know about life here, on our small blue marble in the vastness of space. And here, certain laws of nature rule, laws that enabled life to evolve and ordained that all life would end in death. These always go hand in hand, as two sides of the same coin of nature. These laws apply wherever life might blossom on our planet, in all its amazing and countless forms.

The ebb and flow of life is a challenge to this book's theology. Two basic tenets of this theology are these: first, that everything in the world of nature, when broken down to its most basic building blocks and forces, *emanated* from God's nature and thus reveals aspects of His nature; and second, that God allowed this emanation to occur for certain purposes. These two tenets require us to make sense of the ever-present cycle of life and death in the natural world. In what sense, in other words, did this cycle come from God and what does it reveal about God? That's the challenge we now take up, in the theology of death presented here.

I will admit to a certain bias as I write this chapter. I want to present a theology of death that would help us as we grapple with our own death. The existential novelist and philosopher Albert Camus wrote that death made life meaningless and absurd, and that death therefore challenged us to answer the question, *Why bother?* In his view, this was *the* most important philosophical question facing every human being. *How are we to face up to and accept life on its own terms?* This question warrants a theological answer, in my view. That's what this chapter aims to offer.

Any theology of death must be grounded on what death is and why it happens, so let's start by addressing those questions. We will then turn to how the ebb and flow of life can be understood as being *of God*—that is, coming from God and revelatory about God.

First: What is Death?

It is easy to say that death is the cessation of life. Biology can tell us what life is,[1] and when this thing called "life" ends, that's death. Since all living creatures are composed of cells that are alive, as defined biologically, we can say that death is cellular death. Living creatures die, in other words, when their cells die.

In addition to thinking of death as the cessation of life, we might also think of death as a biological event that ends a creature's existence. That is, when a creature that was alive meets its death, it no longer exists. It did not "pass away," as that phrase implies that it passed or transitioned to a different place in a more spiritual form. Rather, in the conceptualization I am suggesting, it passed into nothingness or nonexistence. Philosophically, we can say it passed into nonbeing. The creature was a living being, and when it dies, it is no longer that being. Nor is it any other type of being. It is not "being" anything. It has lost its *beingness*. The creature's body can still exist, but this body no longer houses the living being that the creature was.

Thus, the cycle of life and death can be seen as the *coming into existence* when a creature is born and a *going out of existence* when the creature dies. I think this conceptualization of life and death is relevant to our theological task—that is, to figure out how the ebb and flow of existence itself comes from God.

Next: Why Death Happens

Just as biology can help us understand what death is, it also sheds light on why it happens. Living creatures are composed of living cells and, as I mentioned above, they die when their cells die. Cell death is caused by two main

---

1. Weber, "Life."

processes: apoptosis and necrosis.[2] The first is also called programmed cell death, wherein a cell provokes its own demise in response to a stimulus. Extreme temperature changes or exposure to toxins, for example, can cause a stress response within the cell that causes the cell to die. Necrosis, on the other hand, is cell death that results from injury or infection.

Cells also die, of course, when the organisms in which they live are killed by predators, disease, or old age. In such cases, the cells do not die first, causing the death of the organism. Rather, the organism as a whole dies, and so do the cells that make up the organism.

Death also happens because of entropy, which is a law of physics that affects the universe as a whole and everything within it. The universe is alive with energy, a force that makes things happen or, in the language of physics, performs the "work" of the universe. That's how physics defines what energy is. It's a definition that focuses on what energy does but skirts the question of what energy essentially is. Yes, it's defined as a force, but that tells us little about the nature of this force. What is it made of, for example, and what sort of force is it that enables it to do its work?

The work of energy always creates a certain order wherever that work is done. Before atoms came into existence, their eventual constituent particles were just buzzing about, aimlessly. Then, when energy enters in, the particles are ordered in a way that make the atom. This same process is seen in the ordering of molecules that make a cell, the ordering of cells to make a bodily organ, and the ordering of organs to make a living being. Over time, however, energy weakens or is used up as it performs work, and is eventually dissipated as heat. The order it had maintained breaks down, so atoms decay and cells die. All of this is due to entropy, an inexorable process leading to ever-increasing *dis*order.

The work of energy is grounded in the laws of energy. These laws stipulate that the constituent parts of every whole entity must be ordered in such a way as to create the entity in question. This ordering is what energy does, but it is not done for free. It uses energy, and this energy is used up over time.

It can be misleading to say that energy is "used up," as this implies that the energy is gone. But energy is never destroyed, as we know from the first law of thermodynamics (see below). It is better to say that energy outlives its usefulness. Eventually, it is dissipated as heat when it can no longer perform the ordering referred to above.

It can also be misleading to say the universe is alive with energy. It is more precise, as we learned from Albert Einstein, to say the universe *is* energy. The matter or mass we see in the universe is a form of energy. $E=mc^2$ means

---

2. Manning and Zuzel, "Comparison of Types of Cell Death."

energy and mass are equivalent and interchangeable as two manifestations of the same thing. Saying the universe is energy is similar, in the theology of this book, to saying the universe is *of God*. This is because the energy in the universe came from God and is a manifestation of God's nature.

The way this energy behaves is captured in the laws of thermodynamics.[3] The first law states that the energy in the universe cannot be destroyed, it only changes the form it takes. The second law is about entropy.

Because the energy that sustains life is doing the necessary work within a living organism, and because this energy cannot do this indefinitely, immortality is impossible. Energy itself is immortal, as we know from the first law of thermodynamics. In this book's theology, *Energy is the immortal spirit of God in all things*. The organisms enlivened by this energy, however, are ordained by the laws of energy to perish over time. This is why atoms decay on their own and why cells eventually die on their own if they do not succumb to injury or disease. I will say more about this when I discuss the death of human cells.

Many astrophysicists believe that entropy will eventually lead to the "heat death" of the universe.[4] This means that all the energy in the universe will be dissipated as heat and will no longer be available in atoms (or cells) to do the work that this energy had earlier accomplished. Entropy is also relevant to the discussion that follows, on how death in the universe is *of God*.

Finally, How Does Life and Death Come from God?

Let me return to our basic question: Why has nature, which ultimately came from God, given rise to life forms that are doomed to perish?

In chapter 1, I speculated that God knew the makeup of His nature before willing it to become the fundamentals of our world—that is, the basic building blocks and forces of the universe that our physicists believe originated in the big bang. And I speculated that He did this so the goodness, beauty, and love that were intrinsic to His nature would flourish in the created world. This was God's purpose in the creation, as I conjectured in chapter 2. This background helps to sharpen the question we now need to consider if we are to appreciate how life and death are *of God*. In other words, if life and death came from God, what aspects of God's nature were a spark for life coupled with the inevitability of death?

Of course, no one can answer that question with certitude. I just want us to appreciate that this is *the* question for a theology of death that seeks to

3. Schneider and Sagan, *Into the Cool*.
4. Hawking, *Theory of Everything*, 77–102.

understand how death could be *of God*. It is a question that is relevant for us too as our own death draws near. It can help us accept our death and be at peace with it, to arrive at an acceptance and peace because we can place our death in the larger scheme of things, a scheme that is good and beautiful and loving. We can feel that God holds us as we die and folds our goodness, beauty, and love into Himself and the universe instilled with His purposes.

In what follows, I want to tackle four theological questions about life and death in general before moving on to our human mortality.

1. *God, Energy, and the Source of Life*

Before the creation, I believe God was aware of an intrinsic, purpose-driven energy in His nature. In creating the universe, He set this energy free and it enlivened the entire universe. He did not create this energy; He found that His own nature was imbued with it, that it was a pulsating and abounding energy, perhaps eager to show what it could do. The laws of thermodynamics, discovered by physicists billions of years later, have told us much about this energy, about what it can do and how it behaves.

God's energy in the universe, I believe, has a teleological dimension, a goal toward which it aims. It is instilled with an *impetus toward life* and aims to create the conditions for life's enhancement. This is what God's energy has done. We can therefore infer a purpose or goal within this energy. This goal was at work in the big bang and the stars it created. These stars converted hydrogen into helium through nuclear fusion, and this process gave off light and heat. Large stars eventually ran out of hydrogen and collapsed on themselves, imploding as supernovas and injecting into space certain elements that had been made inside the star, and these elements were pulled together by gravity to form planets. So we ended up with a universe consisting of stars and planets, and the energy from at least one star, our sun, initiated a long process on Earth involving photosynthesis and the evolution of simple one-celled animals.[5]

The impetus toward life (which we could also call a spark or force) we see in the universe had to have a source, and in this book's theology, the source is found in God's nature and in God's will for the impetus toward life to abound in His creation. And because it came from God, this life-driven force went hand in hand with His purposes. Life would be good and beautiful and loving, as much as conditions would allow. Some of these conditions

---

5. Hazen, *Story of Earth*. Gimbel, "Origin of Life," lecture 27 in *Redefining Reality*, 188–94. I am including this citation because of the concise summary it offers of the complicated process that gave rise to life on earth.

flowed seamlessly from God and thus created fertile soil for the fulfillment of His purposes. But other conditions were deleterious because of random forces, forces that could and sometimes did result in evil, ugliness, and hate.

Death itself, however, is not due to randomness. It results everywhere from the laws of energy (see below), just as life does. These laws are seen in how energy behaves. It has fostered life and propelled it forward. We see this in how the initial impetus toward life drew upon the energy that was available in the universe, and how the subsequent evolution of life continued to be fed by this energy. This energy ultimately came from God and is meant to foster His purposes. All living beings owe their existence to this energy. It provided the initial spark and the sustaining power. There would be no life in the universe were it not for this energy and the laws that inform it.

2. God, Energy, and the Cycle of Life and Death

How does death enter this picture? It also results from energy's laws, laws that do not allow energy to sustain any living being indefinitely. Because of entropy, energy wears down in its life-sustaining work and is eventually dissipated as heat. As I mentioned, this is the second law of thermodynamics at work.

The first law of thermodynamics, on the other hand, dictates that energy is never destroyed. When any life ends, the energy that had sustained it flows back to the pool of energy from which life evolves. This cycle of energy is *of God* through and through. This cycle entails the calling forth of life from the pool of energy and the calling back of life to replenish the pool for the furtherance of life. This process of coming forth and coming back is endemic and intrinsic to God's energy in the universe. God knew this would be so, that energy coming forth to sustain life was good, and that energy coming back through death was also good.

The aim of this process, as mentioned above, is to create life and advance life toward ever-increasing fulfillment. In process theology, this is called the creative advance in the universe, a creative advance that is *of God*.[6]

We can relate to this process by considering the evolution that created us. In the long chain of evolution, certain survival advantages were selected and promulgated, and yet all of our progenitors eventually died, as the process of evolution required. Evolution called them forth with characteristics for life's furtherance, and then evolution called them back to place these characteristics in the genetic pool for future generations. The cycle of life and death in evolution is *of God*.

6. Peters, *Creative Advance*.

When we die, we are being called back: that is, the energy that sustains us is being called back to be available for life's furtherance. This is what death is essentially for. It has a purpose that derives from the dynamics of energy in God.

By analogy, we can think of God's energy as the ocean, and we can think of all life forms (including us) as waves on this ocean. We come from God's energy, just as waves come from the ocean, and when we die our energy flows back into God, just as waves eventually flow back to the ocean from which they came.

There is also a certain rationality to the ubiquitous reality of death. Because living space and the resources for life are limited, immortality is not sustainable.[7] Death is logically necessary. I am mentioning this because I believe God is a rational being; the ever-present mortality in the world of nature could reflect the rationality of God that informs the universe.

3. God and Horrible Deaths in the Real World

Thus far, the theology of death presented here pertains only to deaths that occur naturally and peacefully by the laws of energy, not to the way death often or usually happens in the real world. In a perfect world, death would always result from causal laws that are *of God* because they are derived from God and manifest His goodness. And yet so many deaths have other causes, as so many life forms can attest. Death can occur from injury or disease, from predators, from environmental calamities, from starvation, from deformities, and so forth. It appears that countless living beings die horrible deaths. There are a myriad of causal forces behind these deaths, many of which are random and do not carry God's goodness. Instead, they show the havoc wrought from the randomness in the universe. The *specific ways* that death happens, in other words, are far from being *of God*.

There is an important theological distinction here: randomness comes from God but is not willed by God because He could foresee the evil it would cause. It is in the universe only because it was and is a given in God's nature to begin with it. Goodness, beauty, and love, on the other hand, while also givens in God's nature, are empowered by His will to prevail over the evil caused by randomness, including the evil of horrible deaths.

---

7. Williams, "Makropulos Case."

4. God, Randomness, and Suffering

Let me summarize what I've said so far before moving on to our final question. We first saw that life came to be because the necessary spark toward life was part of God and then became a force in nature after the big bang. But life always ends in death: it occurs naturally from the laws of energy, as living beings die on their own, or it occurs traumatically from the random evil in the world. All death is *of* God: the laws of energy come from God, as do the random forces in the universe. And yet I believe God hates the suffering that comes with death.

If this is so, then we can ask: Why does God allow the suffering that He hates? Why didn't He create a universe wherein death would *only* be natural and painless? Why isn't human nature instilled with an unwavering acceptance of death?

These are vexing theological questions, and yet the response of this book's theology has been mentioned in previous chapters. God was powerful enough to bring the universe into being, but not powerful enough to create a perfect universe. A perfect universe would be ruled solely by His goodness. It would embody an unbroken causal chain from His goodness to good outcomes everywhere. But God's universe is not perfect. The casual chain is infected with randomness, and the real world is ruled by laws of physics and biology. Although these laws can be traced back to God's nature, as their ultimate source, the real-world consequences of these laws reflect the randomness in the real world. This randomness can also be traced back to God's nature.

In this book's theology, God willed the universe into being, but not the randomness that has messed things up. This randomness was and is part of the package. As I mentioned before, it originated from God's nature, as did the goodness, beauty, and love that abound in the universe and will, in God's vision, outweigh the negative effects of randomness. I don't believe God's attitude about the tug-of-war between goodness and randomness was simply, "Well, we'll see what happens." Rather, He believed, first of all, that His goodness would win out, and second, this belief is instilled in nature as a force to fulfill the belief.

God's belief is housed in His mind, and God's mind permeates His creation and shapes how thing are. When Albert Einstein pondered the workings of physics, he said he wanted to grasp the mind of God. It is a mystery, I believe, as to how something that is nonphysical (as God's mind must be) can affect the physical world.[8] God's mind must be far superior and far more powerful than our minds.

Perhaps there is a clue to God's mind in quantum entanglement.[9] Particles that were once part of a pair become entangled in such a way that if one particle in the pair is separated from the other, even if placed in a distant corner of the universe, a change in that particle's behavior will *instantaneously* be seen in the behavior of its pair. Physics does not understand how this could be so, as it implies a faster-than-light communication between entangled particles. Perhaps this is akin to the mind of God, which must be everywhere. Thus, a thought or belief in His mind would have immediate, instantaneous effects everywhere, throughout the universe as a whole.

God and Human Mortality

I have been discussing how the life and death of living beings in the world of nature can be seen as stemming from God's nature and will. This applies to us, of course, but I have not specifically addressed our *human* experience—first of living with our mortality, and then eventually dying. It's one thing to discuss how the ebb and flow of life, in the abstract, is *of God*, but what about our lived experience of death? How is that *of God*? Let's turn to that now.

In chapter 6, I put forth the idea that God was a person-like being in our innermost depth, and I posited that this God cares about us. He knows we must live with the knowledge that we will eventually die, and He cares about the impact of our knowing this on our overall well-being. And He cares about the manner of our eventual death, about what it will be like for us.

Earlier, I addressed how death in the natural world can be *of God*. Does this apply to our deaths too? The fact that we must die can be traced back to God and reveals aspects of God's nature. So yes, our deaths are *of God* in that sense.

But our deaths warrant a separate discussion because our mortality and our dying are realities we *experience* as conscious beings. We don't know if this is true of other life forms. We don't even know if this is true of our beloved pets. But we know it is true for human beings, so we have to ask, if we want to grasp a theology of death that applies to us: Where is God in our *experience* of life and death?

---

8. God's *desire* for life to evolve, for example, was not a *physical* force; it was a spiritual force that was able to bring about the physical conditions for life to evolve.

9. Clegg, *God Effect*, 2–5.

It is not only *our* mortality and death that we experience, however. We also experience the death of our loved ones, and the deaths of our fellow humans on a colossal scale. So often, these are the vast numbers of war casualties and the dying children (from wars, starvation, or disease) that we witness on the nightly news. Any theology of death must apply to these deaths too. I sought to do that in our last chapter, on the problem of evil.

I mentioned cellular death earlier, in the previous section on why death happens in the natural world. Cellular death applies to us too. We die because our cells die.[10] A main reason for the death of our cells is lack of oxygen. Our cells require oxygen to live, and this oxygen is delivered through the blood stream. Blood flow to our cells can be fatally curtailed or stopped by injury to vital organs or from a number of illnesses, most notably diseases of the heart.

Our cells can also die from infection and toxic exposure. These causes of cell death are considered out of the ordinary or accidental; they are not ordained as inevitable for everyone.

Another cause of cell death, however, is considered natural because it results, over time, from the normal process of cell division.[11] Each time a cell divides, its chromosomes are copied and passed on to the daughter cells. But each time this happens, the very ends of chromosomes (called telomeres) are not copied. Once the telomeres shrink to a critical minimum size, enough genetic information has been lost to destabilize the chromosome, resulting in cell aging and death. If we are fortunate enough to escape all the diseases and malfunctions that can curtail life-giving blood flow to our cells, this natural process will bring our death in due time.

It is also thought that natural selection has programmed us to die.[12] Mortality assures that the resources necessary for the survival of descendants would be available for them. It therefore promotes the survival advantage of our species. This perspective suggests that while death may be bad for us as individuals, it is actually good for the human race as a whole.

Earlier, I speculated that the death of living beings was the end of their existence. I believe this applies to our existence as well. Of course, our bodies do not cease to exist when we die, but the self that we are, a self that lives by virtue of the body being alive, that self ceases to exist when the body and its brain die. I say that because our conscious sense of self is created by our brains, so when our brains cease to function, we cease to be. (I realize this may not be true, and that our consciousness may survive our bodily

---

10. Wolpert, *How We Live and Why We Die.*
11. Saltsman, "The Last Chapter: Cell Aging and Death."
12. Werfel et al., "Programed Death."

death.[13] The evidence for this is not compelling, in my view, nor are the theories about consciousness that support this idea.)

Our Lived Experience of Being Mortal

As I mentioned previously, I want to move on from what death is and why it happens to addressing how we *experience* our mortality. The experience of anything, of course, is an individual matter. While each of us is having to live with being mortal,[14] and while the circumstances of each death are individual, and while everyone experiences their death in a personal way, I believe certain aspects of our experience are common, and I have sought to describe some of these aspects in what follows.

You will notice that what I have written below seems unnecessarily grim or harsh. I will comment on this toward the end of this section. Please bear with me for now.

Our experience of death starts, in my view, with the knowledge of our mortality and later progresses to actually dying. I will have less to say about the dying process as this has been so keenly described in a highly-regarded book on the ways we die.[15]

Our first awakening to the experience of death comes when the fact of our mortality first dawns on us. This knowledge introduces us to a troubling truth, a truth that can bring a jolting dismay and trepidation. Because of the profound implications of this truth, it normally sinks into our consciousness gradually instead of hitting us immediately. We each struggle in our own way to come to terms with our mortality. Our initial experience of it is in our minds only. It is not a bodily experience. Most of us were young and healthy when we first learned of it, and yet at that moment, a disquieting and ominous truth infiltrated our young minds.

Over the course of our lives, after the initial jolt fades, the troubling truth of our eventual death stays with us. It is stark and unrelenting, gnawing at us deep in our minds. There is no escaping the existential anxiety and dread that comes with this knowledge.[16] Denying it or trying not to think about it can help us be happy or content with life on its own terms, but these defenses do not totally work. I think Freud was right in what he said about this kind of denial: part of the ego knows the truth.

---

13. Laszlo, *Immortal Mind*.
14. Gawande, *Being Mortal*.
15. Nuland, *How We Die*, 42, 123.
16. Tillich, *Courage to Be*, 40–45.

Earlier, I suggested a certain understanding of what death is, that it's the end of our existence. Referring to Freud again, he famously said that no one really believes it, for it's too unfathomable to realize that our very existence will be wiped away, that we will cease to be, and that our death will be final. Some people feel that not existing is hardly a problem, just as they did not exist before they were born. But still, there can be something jarring about the fact that we will be forgotten and lost forever. I say "forgotten" because there will come a day when no one will even know we existed. And I say "lost" because *we* will be lost, the person we are, what we've made of ourselves, what we have to contribute—certainly to our loved ones and perhaps to society or mankind as a whole—all of this will eventually be lost. All we have done with our lives will eventually amount to nothing. All the thoughts and feelings that we hold dear will die with us. All the memories we cherish will also perish. With the passing of time, mankind as a whole will lose us. And mankind as a whole will eventually be lost, along with everything else, with the expected death of the universe.[17]

Losing our lives, and being lost and forgotten—this is what the knowledge of our mortality confronts us with.

Among the many ways that our mortality causes us to suffer, mentally and emotionally, is the way our death is forced upon us. We are forced to live with a kind of death sentence.[18] It's a defining aspect of the human condition. It is the price that must be paid for getting to live, and for many, this price is detestable. It's part of the deal, in other words, and yet we are never asked if we accept this deal, we were never invited to enter into it voluntarily.

Besides being forced upon us, death also comes (for most people) at the wrong time. We can be confronted with it quite suddenly, long before we are ready or have time to prepare. It is especially jolting, of course, for those who receive a life-threatening diagnosis when they are relatively young. Even if elderly, people can be enjoying a good quality of life and not feel ready to face the end. They can feel they had so much to look forward to or so much unfinished business to attend to.

Some people are especially revolted by the harsh reality of death because of a sense of self-importance or grandiosity. They secretly expect a special death because they are special. By a special death, I mean a death that comes at the right time and in a peaceful fashion. "I don't expect a lot of suffering when my time comes," a patient told me. In reality, of course, death happens to a body and does not care about the person or the person's sense of entitlement to a peaceful passing.

17. Hawking, *Theory of Everything*, 77–102.
18. Gawande, *Being Mortal*, 8, 25–54.

Much of what I have written above is relevant to those of us in developed countries. The majority of us have had a decent life, a life that helps us come to terms with the inevitable end. Many or even most of our fellow humans, however, have not enjoyed the luxury of balancing the starkness of death with the richness of life. For many, their life has been one of deprivation and suffering. They have seen their children wither and heave as they starve to death. In Africa, countless children have died of AIDS. The relentless suffering of so many people in India has caused them to look at death as a welcome relief. In any event, most have not had the luxury of thinking philosophically, much less theologically, about their ultimate fate.

Living with our mortality is one thing, while actually being confronted with really dying is another can of worms. Death can come for us in many different ways, and as I already said, it rarely comes at the right time or in a peaceful fashion.[19] Even if we accept the inevitability of death, and accept (in our saner moments) that immortality makes no sense,[20] we are still confronted with the physical and emotional suffering that death brings.

Dying confronts us with a defining aspect of our existence—namely, that we are simply biological creatures, and this basic truth is something that we are all challenged to come to terms with. Mentally, we can think that we *have* bodies, which shields us from the fact that we essentially *are* bodies.[21] When we are in good health, we can live mostly in our minds. When we are ill, on the other hand, our basic creatureliness takes center stage and we become preoccupied with our physical state. Illness and our approaching death can force us to face up to what we really are.

The body that we are abides by its own laws of cause and effect, laws that can be indifferent to what we think or want. Earlier, I spoke of the laws of energy that apply to life and death. These laws govern the process of energy utilization, which accounts for life, and the process of energy expenditure, which accounts for our eventual death. These mindless, lawful processes have no regard for us.

I realize what I have written sounds quite grim. Not everyone, to be sure, experiences their mortality in these bleak terms. Many people are at peace with it long before they die, and then face their actual death with courage and dignity. I have not wanted to sugar coat the experience of

---

19. Nuland, *How We Die*. In this book, Dr. Nuland discusses six common biological causes of death, noting that the idea of a peaceful death is largely a myth.

20. Williams, "Makropulos Case."

21. Becker, *Denial of Death*. This Pulitzer Prize–winning book is only indirectly about the denial of death. It is mostly about the denial of our basic creatureliness, something that is so difficult for us to accept.

death, however, as I know too well the suffering it can bring.[22] Moreover, I have wanted to call a spade a spade when it comes to the stark aspects of death because, as I said at the beginning, any theology of death should grapple with what death is and how it is commonly experienced.

Because I am formulating a theology of death, I want to lay *our* experience of death at God's feet, as if to challenge Him and plead with Him. Why does it have to be this bad? I know it's not always as harsh as I've laid out. But why does it *ever* have to be this bad? Why does *any* child have to starve to death? These are essential and vexing questions for theology, and in this book's theology, there is no letting God off the hook.

God's Response to Our Mortality

As you already know, the theology of this book does not blame God for our suffering and death. He did not design the universe to be the way it is and He lacks the power to intervene to make things better. He is not a designer God and He did not instill an intelligent design in the universe. The universe flowed from His nature and He did not create His own nature. His nature was a mixture of the ingredients and forces that would create a world of goodness, beauty, and love, but random forces were also present, and these forces could create evil, ugliness, and love. Yes, I've already discussed all that.

My topic now concerns God's person-like response to our suffering and death. This is all conjecture, of course, but it's conjecture based on a sound theology. I believe God responds to our suffering with a depth of sorrow and compassion that far exceeds what we can imagine. God's emotional life is not like ours. It is far richer, both in happiness and in sorrow. We cannot fathom how God feels. But if we believe in the God of love, then we can certainly postulate that this God suffers when the living beings He loves meet an untimely or gruesome death.

God's suffering is complicated, I believe. As a spiritual being, He does not suffer physically. His suffering is akin to the unbearable heartache we experience when a person we love is injured or killed. We suffer internally, in such cases. Our pain is inside us, and this is also true, I believe, of the pain God feels.

---

22. As I mentioned in my acknowledgments, after studying theology in graduate school, I was lured away by a desire to work as a clinical psychologist with people who were afflicted with cancer. I did this for over thirty years at the University of California, San Francisco (UCSF), Comprehensive Cancer Center. After I retired, I sought to pass along what I had learned from the patients there in my first book, *Finding Your Way through Cancer*.

God also suffers from profound regret. All human suffering results from a causal chain that goes back to an ultimate or first cause, which is the randomness in God's nature. That wasn't God fault, but He regrets it to the depths of His being. And He regrets that He lacks the power to abolish all untimely or gruesome deaths. He wishes He could do more to help, but here's the point: He resides within the innermost depth of every person who suffers and is a never-ending and never-depleted resource for goodness, beauty, and love. I will return to this point in the final chapter of this book.

Earlier, I spoke of the all the gruesome, horrific, and untimely ways that death can come for us. In a perfect world, the chain of causality from God would only lead to deaths that were timely and due to natural causes. Such deaths would be *of God*, as I have said many times. But in the real world things are not perfect. The causal chain is disrupted by random forces. Many such disruptions can be benign or neutral, but many can also cause horrific suffering, such as the birth defects that results from random mutations. While randomness itself is *of God*, I don't believe this is true of the horrible *manifestations* of randomness in the created world. Such deaths were not foreseen by God, in the act of creation, and are not willed by God.

In a certain sense, God and human beings are in the same boat. The capriciousness of nature is a problem for us both. And yet God's way of confronting this problem is unflinching and wise, and He has imparted this to us. He empowers us to follow His lead.

How Can God Help Us?

In the previous section I conjectured about the how and why of God's suffering. Now I want to tackle how God masters His suffering. To put this question in human terms that we can relate to: How is it that God's suffering never gets the best of Him? The way God helps Himself reveals how His spirit, in the depth of our being, can help us in dealing with our own suffering.

God places His suffering in the broadest possible context and brings to His suffering the broadest possible perspective. *Context* and *Perspective*. These are key components of God's way, and His spirit empowers us to follow His lead.

Context and perspective are inherently linked. No event happens in total isolation from what came before it or from what is likely to stem from it. This is the context in which the event occurs. The meaning of an event is anchored in its context. It is important to place an event in its proper context so that our response to it can be appropriate (fitting and warranted, given the context).

A proper context is fearless in the sense that it encompasses all relevant aspects, regardless of their implications. If someone has hurt our feelings in the past, and then does so again, the most recent hurt occurs in the context of the past hurts. This could cause us to respond to the most recent hurt with *more* anger or bitterness than would otherwise be the case. On the other hand, if this person had never hurt our feelings in the past, then does so on one occasion, we could be more likely to forgive that one hurt.

Placing an event in its proper context is very similar to having a broad perspective on it. Perspective refers to our point of view. If we step back from something, a broad perspective takes in the big picture, even if aspects of this picture are not consistent. A broad perspective aims to integrate conflicting aspects.

These notions about context and perspective apply to God, and they also apply to us. When God is confronted with the evil that results from random forces, He places this evil in its *proper context* and brings the *broadest of perspectives* to it.

For God, the proper context encompasses all the evil and all the good in His creation. As I've said many times, He believes the good will outweigh the evil when the final tally is taken at the end of time. So, when a particular evil is staring Him in the face—a young child dying from cancer, for example—He faces that evil head on and is painfully distraught over it. It impacts Him because it is evil in its own right. And yet He also places this evil occurrence alongside all the goodness, beauty, and love in His creation. In this context, the particular evil confronting Him does not cause Him to lose hope. He believes His purposes will prevail in the long run.

God also takes the broadest of all possible perspectives. He apprehends everything that came before an evil event and everything that could result from it. His perspective also takes in all the goodness, beauty, and love in His creation, which also frames the proper context for His response, as mentioned above. All of this shapes the big picture for God. This big-picture perspective enables God to respond to evil in a way that is balanced and fitting.

When we are confronted with evil of any kind, we are challenged to harness the spirit of God that dwells within us. And yet what, specifically, does it mean for us to place something that's evil in its proper context and to bring a broad perspective to it?

First, the evil we encounter would have an impact on us that is commensurate with the evilness in question. This is what God does and He empowers us to do likewise, as best we can. Thus, we would not downplay or deny the evil confronting us.

Second, we would step back from this evil in order to take in the big picture. The big picture would encompass all the evils and all the goodness, beauty, and love in our lives. These would be pitted against each other so that the proper balance could be attained. This is also what God does.

The evil we encounter and the suffering it causes can defeat our spirit, but only if we are mindless of all the ways we have not suffered. It is our gratitude for every small blessing in our lives that puts our suffering in its proper place. This perspective and gratitude is God's spirit, alive within us. This is how God can help us.

Of course, the impact of evil on us, and our ability to apprehend the big picture, pale in comparison to the impact on God and to the big picture He can take in. The impact on God must exceed our capacity to comprehend, and His perspective must encompass aspects that we are not even aware of. But still, we are not on our own in dealing with evil. God's spirit is in us for a reason.

The broad context of the suffering life throws at us, including our having to die, is that we got to live in the first place. We got to experience all the wondrous aspects of our existence. Being mindful of this, and resolutely grateful, will render all the ways we suffer less onerous and less defeating of the human spirit that beats within us (ch. 10). We do not need to believe in the God of this book's theology to do this; we can still balance the suffering of death with gratitude for getting to live. In the theology presented here, however, this gratitude reflects the spirit of God, alive within us.

Emily Dickinson wrote: "Just to live is so startling it hardly leaves time for anything else." The more we are aware of this quality, the greater our gratitude would be. And yet being alive is something we tend to take for granted. This would not be so if we were in a coma since birth and then *suddenly* came out of the coma and found ourselves being alive; our five senses alone would be astounding to us. By analogy, people blind from birth can learn to navigate through their home and around their neighborhood, but then, if their sight is restored, they find themselves speechless in actually *seeing* the world in which they had been living. These examples underscore how much more grateful we would be for getting to live if we were not so used to being alive. My point is that we can more easily balance the pain of saying goodbye to life with gratitude for getting to live in the first place if we are more fully aware of how unspeakably exhilarating it is to be alive.

Sometimes people are so sick they wished they were dead. In this book's theology, God's compassion would be wrapped around them, and if

He could, He would grant their wish and hasten their demise. God would not want their suffering to continue. But He would not want them to forget all the times they were not sick. Gratitude for getting to live in the first place packs enormous, transformative power. This is a testament to God's spirit in the ground of our being.

10

A Theology of the Human Spirit

Our previous chapter took up the question of death, which is ever-present in God's world. Because it is endemic in the book of nature, it must (according to the theology we've been exploring) come from God and reveal something about God. And yet also ever-present in God's world, on our planet at least, is the astounding capacity of the human spirit in confronting death and all the other ways we inevitably suffer. Our human spirit shines bright in the resilience, perseverance, and fortitude we find in ourselves, and also in our capacity for gratitude and perspective. Our suffering is not the *only* given of our existence; also given to us is the goodness, beauty, and love that have blessed our lives. Not allowing our suffering to obliterate this is also the human spirit at work.

When we take stock of the many manifestations of the human spirit, certain theological questions present themselves, just as they did when we considered the reality of death. The power of the human spirit must have a *source*; that's our first question. And when we see the human spirit in action, what might it reveal about this source? That's the second question.

I will focus here on two ways the human spirit manifests itself, as these will help us in addressing the two questions posed above. The first manifestation falls under the heading of *Our Resilience*. I believe we have all experienced our capacity for resilience more than once in our lives. These manifestations of the human spirit can be considered *ordinary*, as distinct from the *extraordinary* manifestations that we take up next. These fall under the heading of *Turning Straw into Gold*, which I will explain shortly. These manifestations reveal the transformative power of the human spirit in the most trying of circumstances.

I will give just three examples of turning straw into gold. I believe these real-life examples are powerful illustrations of what the human spirit can do when we are pushed to our limits. While these examples only scratch the surface, they are sufficient to illustrate the theology of the human spirit under consideration.

Our Resilience

The boundless resilience of the human spirit has been ubiquitous in the history of our species. It is also a resounding force in each of us. We each carry the power of this resilience inside of us. It may seem asleep at times, but is never gone for good. Oftentimes, we need it desperately, and oftentimes it will come forth. It can make sense to actually pray for it. We would not be praying to a transcendent God and we would not be asking for Him to intervene in our lives. In this book's theology, as you know from what I've written before, it is not in God's nature or wherewithal to intervene in human history. And yet God's spirit is alive in us, in the ground of our being, and we can pray to it to come forth with power and resolve.

We all need to bounce back from the disappointments, heartaches, and challenges life throws at us. Life is not a cakewalk for anyone. No one is perfectly healthy, in body and mind. No one is completely satisfied with his or her body just the way it is. No one's mind is free of confusion, anxiety, self-doubt. No one is completely happy all the time. Life is not *always* difficult and disquieting, of course, but it certainly is *sometimes*.

And yet the hardships of life are countered by our resilience. Not always, of course, but often, perhaps usually. We don't let our misfortunes define us or ruin our lives. In the following list, I offer some examples of the ways we bounce back. As you read these, some items will not apply to you because you have not had to be resilient in those specific ways. But other items will certainly ring true. While a specific item may or may not apply to you, each one speaks to the capacity for resilience that we each possess.

- Instead of hating our bodies when we are sick, as with a relentless cold or flu, we remind ourselves that we are usually healthy and love our bodies for that.

- Instead of losing hope, when a serious illness strikes, we rally against it with our inner strength and get the help we need.
- Instead of feeling damaged and unlovable—because of a series of rejections, for example, or a painful divorce—we remember the unwavering love that many people have for us.
- Instead of being preoccupied by regret over a poor decision—pertaining to our occupation or a specific job, for example—we forgive ourselves (we are only human, after all) and think of life decisions we do not regret.
- Instead of not being able to accept a painful loss—be it the loss of a loved one, a home, a pet, a job—we grieve fully until we can come to terms with the loss we have suffered.
- Instead of ceaselessly protesting the unfairness of life, we remind ourselves of all the ways life has been kind to us.
- Instead of being gripped by resentment, when someone offends us, we are gripped by compassion for the offending person, recognizing they have been injured or offended themselves.
- Instead of reproaching ourselves for not living up to our ideals, we love ourselves in spite of our shortcomings.
- Instead of being preoccupied by bodily features that we wish were different, we love ourselves the way we are.
- Instead of hating being alive when it is senselessly cruel to us, we love the gift of life in spite of the suffering it has brought to us.
- Instead of holding ourselves back, when our goals in life seem unreachable, we forge ahead by embracing the gifts and aspirations we find in ourselves.
- Instead of abusing alcohol or other drugs in response to the stresses of life, we find more positive ways of reducing these stresses and seek help in combating addiction.
- Instead of taking it personally and feeling hurt when our personal needs seem overlooked by others, we strive to overcome our grandiosity and self-importance.
- Instead of allowing our deficiencies to define and limit us, we appreciate and are empowered by the real strengths we possess.

- Instead of suppressing our sorrow, when we are injured bodily or by a broken heart, we cry as much as we need to, until we need to cry no more.
- Instead of putting ourselves down, in comparison to those who are more accomplished, we find value and self-esteem in reaching goals that are important to *us*.
- Instead of questioning the value of life, when it seems to lack meaning or purpose, we love life anyway and create our own meaning.
- Instead of clinging desperately to life when terminally ill, we accept that it's time to let go, and do that peacefully, perhaps knowing that we have loved and been loved.

These manifestations of resilience speak to its power, and no one, I believe, is intrinsically deprived of this power. It can be dormant in our souls for many years, but eventually it will come to life and empower us to bounce back. My basis for saying this is found in the theology presented in this book. *The depth of our being is of God: it comes from God and carries God's spirit and purposes.* This depth within us is the source of our resilience. God's spirit is alive and active in this depth.

Let's turn to the second question I posed at the outset. What does our resilience reveal about God? This can be seen in the intrinsic *purpose* of our resilience. What is it there *for*? What does it accomplish? What are its objectives?

In every case, our resilience emerges as a response to a difficulty posed by life. It never negates this difficulty. It accepts it as given. But resilience *balances* it with something good. The "badness" of a serious illness, for example, and the badness of the despair or resignation it can foster, is balanced by the hope and tenacity of rallying against it. This makes the illness less bad in what it does to us. It does not intimidate or defeat us. The badness of life's senseless cruelty, to take another example, is balanced by the goodness of our loving life in spite of the suffering it imposes.

What does this reveal about God? The answer is found in God's purposes, as put forth in chapters 2 and 3. God's cause is to balance the badness of randomness with the goodness of His overarching purposes. This is what matters to God—balancing our suffering with what is good and right about us and our lives. Perspective and balance are manifestations of God's spirit, so the downsides of life and all the ways we suffer do not get the upper hand. They do not get the best of us. In our resilience, we get the best of them!

Everywhere in His creation, God's spirit is a force for goodness, beauty, and love. This aspect of God is seen in our resilience to the difficulties inherent to the human condition.

Turning Straw Into Gold

As I mentioned before, this section will deal with some *extraordinary* manifestations of the human spirit—manifestations that reveal the transformative power of the human spirit in the most trying of circumstances. When pushed to our limits, the human spirit often comes forth and shows what it can do, pushing back with awe-inspiring resilience, courage, and self-sacrifice. This pushing back is absolutely stunning in what it reveals about our humanness. If we want to know what we are made of, dig here . . . dig down deep to the ultimate source of turning straw into gold. Surely this will reveal the better angels of our existence.

The straw I am referring to, in the examples that follow, is something horrible that has happened to a person, such as a life-altering injury or disease. The "gold" is the opportunity it presents to do something positive about the source of the horrible thing that has happened. For example, before seat belts were mandatory in cars, a driver lost both legs and one eye in a horrific accident. He then joined the campaign to force Congress to require automakers to install seat belts in all cars. Something good came from his personal misfortune. He turned straw into gold.

A person is healed internally by turning straw into gold, and this healing is part of what the human spirit aims to accomplish. The straw in our life is always a manifestation of our victimhood. We are vulnerable to the dangers that surround us and that lurk within us, and we are victims of these dangers when they occur. We can be victims of accidents, of brutality, or the capriciousness of nature. As victims only, we are powerless. But when we respond to our victimhood with power, with the power of turning the tables, so to speak, we become *victors instead of victims*. As victims we are injured, as victors we are healed. The examples I present will make this clear.

What I said before about the source of our resilience, and what it reveals about that source, applies especially to the power of turning straw into gold.

This power is perhaps the pinnacle of our resilience and reveals the healing force of God's spirit. The power of God, pulsating in the ground of our being, not only aims to balance life's difficulties with something good, beautiful, or loving, as I mentioned when discussing resilience in general. It also aims to heal us internally, perhaps even to redeem us. The straw we encounter in life can make us ask, Why me? Did we deserve it? Did we need to learn a certain lesson from it? Did we need to be put down, to be put in our place? When we turn this straw into gold, we reclaim our essential goodness. This is also what God wants for us.

There are many well-known examples of turning straw into gold.

- Helen Keller, who was blind and deaf since age two, learned to read and speak, earned a college degree, and became an inspiring model for others who were afflicted with severe handicaps.
- Nelson Mandela was imprisoned for his protests against white minority rule and eventually led a successful campaign against apartheid, became South Africa's first democratically-elected president, and was awarded the Nobel Peace Prize in 1993.
- The psychiatrist Viktor Frankl survived three harrowing years at Auschwitz by refusing to give up or give in. The meaning of his suffering was to triumph over it, to not let it defeat his spirit. He later wrote *Man's Search for Meaning*, in which he presented a groundbreaking approach to psychotherapy based on his experience at Auschwitz.
- Malala Yousfzai was shot in the head at age eleven by a Taliban gunman in Pakistan because she advocated for the education of girls, which the Taliban fought to abolish. She clung to life and vowed to continue the cause of education for girls, and was awarded the Nobel Peace Prize in 2014, when she was only seventeen years old.
- Frederick Douglass was born into slavery in 1818, in Talbot County, Maryland. He learned to read and write at age twelve and became a national leader of the abolitionist movement, an early champion of women's rights, and one of the most respected intellectuals of his time.

There are countless other examples of turning straw into gold, but I want to highlight just three of those because they are such powerful manifestations of what the human spirit can do.

The Woman Who Lost Her Face

In 1999, on a country road in Texas, a beautiful twenty-year-old woman was driving home from a birthday party with three friends. She was not beautiful in a glamorous or made-up way; rather, her face was just naturally sweet, charming, and endearing. On her way home, on a two-lane road, a drunk driver swerved into her lane and smashed head-on into her small car. Two of her friends were killed instantly. The fiery inferno that resulted severely burned her body from head to toe. But it was especially her face that bore the brunt of the intense heat. It was virtually burned off. Her lips, eyebrows and eyelids, and nose were completely obliterated. She underwent over one hundred surgeries and skin grafts, but these efforts to repair and restore her face were far from successful. In a word, she was left with a hideous and frightening face.[1] She was profoundly depressed and thought of ending her life.

What she did instead was profoundly moving. She asked herself: What can I do with my face, this face that causes people to look away? The answer that came to her, perhaps from God's spirit in the core of her being, was that her face made a powerful point about the dangers of drunk driving. People know that driving drunk can cause accidents, but that tends to be a general knowledge; the horrifying specifics of what an accident can do to a human body are not widely known. A fast car is like a guided missile. It explodes, kills, and maims on impact. This was the point she wanted to make, and her face would enable her to make it.

She went public with her story and with her repulsive-looking face. Her face appeared in magazines and people were drawn to her story. She gave many high school presentations about drunk driving. She appeared twice on the Oprah Winfrey show. All in all, she became a fearless and tireless advocate for better laws and programs related to drunk driving. She had turned her own tragedy into an opportunity to make a difference on a problem that had cost her her face.

If we search for the sources of her resilience, we can find clues in her personal history, her vibrant personality, and other challenges she had faced. No clues could be found in her religious beliefs, for she had none as far as we know. But this book's theology still applies to her, and we can assert that the ultimate source was God's spirit within her. This God did not need her to believe in Him. He needed nothing from her. He only wanted to help her. But how? Not by miraculously restoring her face, for He lacked the power to do that. But she had the power to tap into her inner resources . . . resources and strengths that came from the ground of her being. They could help her make something good come from her personal tragedy. And this helped to heal her internally, transforming her from victim to victor.

Many times in this book, I have asserted that God is an ever-present source of goodness, beauty, and love in His creation. And we can see this God, this sacred source, at work in this story. It was good what she did with her hideous face. It was no longer beautiful, but there was something

---

1. At the conclusion of this chapter I will present the startling before-and-after photos of her face.

beautiful that she was doing with it. And this caused her to be even more loved and admired.

The Woman with Malignant Melanoma

I know this woman personally from my work in a cancer center before writing this book. She was forty-two years old with auburn hair and a few freckles. She worked for a documentary film studio in San Francisco. She noticed a new mole on her thigh but did not think much about it. It itched only a little. She said it was shaped like a tiny kidney bean as opposed to being perfectly round like her other moles. Other than that it looked normal to her eye; it did not appear mean or nasty or threatening in any way. It was uniformly black; there were no purplish or reddish areas on it, and it certainly didn't ooze or bleed. All in all, it was quite innocent looking.

One morning while shaving her legs she nicked the mole with her razor and it bled so profusely that it took several minutes of direct pressure, and some help with ice cubes, to stop the bleeding. It had completely healed by the next day, but it looked more abnormal, and she was now worried enough about it to make an appointment with a dermatologist. He biopsied the lesion and said the results would be back in five days. She asked what he thought it might be. He said it was too soon to tell but it could be a melanoma.

She had heard that melanoma could be serious, but she did not know how. It was just a tiny, pesky mole on her thigh, and now it was gone. How could this pose any danger?

While she waited for the biopsy results, she read about melanoma online and became increasingly worried. But she also learned that melanomas can be caught early, before spreading into the blood stream, and are therefore completely cured upon removal from the skin.

She was not so fortunate to get that news when she received a call from the dermatologist's office. She was told the biopsy was positive for melanoma, but worse still, it had grown quite deep and the biopsy procedure did not remove it all. A wider and deeper surgery was needed, and for that she needed to see a surgeon who had experience with this type of problem. Even more worrisome, the dermatologist's office had already made an appointment for her to see the surgeon because it was important for the more extensive surgery to be done as soon as possible. Needless to say, all this was greatly alarming.

There was more bad news when she saw the surgeon. When he examined the lymph node area in her groin, he felt one hard lump and she could see the worry on his face. She asked what this could mean and was told the melanoma had probably metastasized to this nodal area. Deep melanomas like hers can invade lymphatic vessels, she was told, and travel that way to lymph nodes in the area. She wanted to know how serious this would be if this had happened in her case. He said that melanoma often spreads to lymph nodes but nowhere else in the body, but that further tests would be needed to determine the outlook in her case. "What do you mean by outlook?" she bravely asked. He said that outlook referred to the fact that melanomas can be cured, but they can also be fatal in the long run. Each case had a certain chance of going either way, he said. Her chances of being cured would be good if the further tests found no indication the cancer had spread beyond the lymph nodes, but there was no way of knowing for sure that this had not happened. That was because melanoma can spread to other organs through the blood stream, but be too microscopic to show up on a scan. Her prognosis, in other words, was uncertain, but still, it was abundantly clear that her life was in danger.

When the surgery was performed, the melanoma on her thigh was completely removed, along with the hardened lymph node in her groin and those adjacent to it. Only that one lymph node was positive for metastatic melanoma. Follow-up scans were clear, indicating that the melanoma may not have spread anywhere else in her body. "Do you think I'm cured?" she bravely asked. "Time will tell," the surgeon said. He explained that follow-up physical exams and scans would be needed over the coming years. She quickly put two and two together, concluding that she'd be living with uncertainty, with the mythical Sword of Damocles over her head.

As she was recovering from the surgery, lying in bed one morning, somehow the most compelling idea came into her mind. She felt she had been tricked by the melanoma, that it looked innocent and nonthreatening at first, as it was secretly growing deep and invading lymphatic vessels to spread to a lymph node and perhaps beyond. But the compelling aspect of this idea, of being tricked, was that many other people can be tricked as well, and that she had the skills and connections to make a difference. Perhaps she could help others not to be tricked like she was.

Her idea was to make a short public service film, perhaps only thirty seconds long, showing a series of photos of benign-looking melanomas on the skin, with each photo followed by bold black letters stating the true diagnosis. She made the film with the help of her friends at work. It was extremely powerful and impossible to miss the message: Don't be tricked by a mole that looks pretty normal. It could kill you.

I asked what led her to make this film. First, she said the idea just came to her. But then she said, becoming choked with emotion as she said it, so that it became a whisper she could barely get out: I wanted something good to come from the bad thing that happened to me. Tears welled up as she struggled to say this, and I asked what she was feeling. It made her sad to think of the bad thing that happened to her, the way she had been victimized by it, but it was moving to think it could be a gift for others. "Maybe somebody will be saved, even if I am not," she said, as more tears flowed.

We see in this the themes we have discussed before, of turning straw into gold, of moving from victim to victor. Once again, we can wonder about the source of the idea that came to her and about the source of her motivation to follow through with it. In this book, we are exploring a theology that sheds light on this question . . . a theology about the sacred source within us.

The Fulfillment of a Rabbi

In the early 1940s, before the mechanized murder of European Jewry began in German-run extermination camps, special German killing squads (the infamous *Einsatzkommandos*) swept through Ukraine, through small towns and villages, gathering all the Jews they could find, herding them out to the surrounding forest, where grave pits had been dug, then shooting them in the back of their heads or machine-gunning them en masse, causing them to fall into the grave they were facing. Men, women, and children were massacred in this way.[2]

Word reached one countryside town that the Germans were approaching, giving the congregation of the local synagogue a chance to hide. The perfect hiding place was a secret basement in their synagogue that could only be reached through a trap door. When the Germans arrived, they rounded up as many Jews as they could find, but suspected there must be many more, as they were told of a rabbi who had a large congregation. They arrested the rabbi and brutally tortured him to reveal where his congregation was hiding.

The rabbi refused to disclose the hiding place, but eventually the torture became so severe and sadistic that he could stand it no longer. He therefore lied, saying his people were hiding in the bombed-out ruins of another temple. He was locked in a dungeon and told the gallows would be awaiting him if his congregation could not be found where he claimed they were hiding.

One of his jailors was a Romanian who was sympathetic to the plight of Jews and risked his life by helping the rabbi to escape, and then directed

---

2. For the history of these atrocities, and for the story of the rabbi presented here, see Desbois, *Holocaust by Bullets*.

him to a secure place to hide, which was his own home. When his congregation could not be found in the ruined temple, the German soldiers returned hot with blood lust, eager to execute the rabbi. When they discovered he had escaped, the jailors present said they did not know how this happened. The Germans had to settle for the Jews they had captured, who were led to the outskirts of town, where a mass grave was waiting.

After the Germans moved on, the rabbi told his congregation that it was safe to come out. Many members left immediately to warn the Jewish communities in other towns, hoping to beat the advancing Germans. The rabbi wanted to help in a different way. He had been stunned by how many townspeople had cooperated with the Germans executioners and was appalled by the depth of latent anti-Semitism that had emerged. This was the underlying problem, he felt, and wanted to do what he could about that.

The wife of the jailor who helped him escape was a teacher in a small local school, and this gave him an idea. He asked if he could visit the school to explain Judaism and who the Jews really were. He realized that many of the non-Jews in his town had a bias against their Jewish neighbors because of Nazi propaganda, especially the myth of the Jewish plan of global domination. There were many other myths about Jews that the Nazis wanted people to believe, and the rabbi wanted to counter those with a correct history of the Jewish people, their true religious beliefs, their innate character, and their many contributions to society. Of course, he would need to conceal his true identity; otherwise, he would be sure to be found out and reported to the Nazis who had stayed in town to murder any Jews who could be found. His plan was obviously dangerous, but he was committed to it nonetheless.

After his first visit to the school, many of the teachers invited him to return every few days because they appreciated what he had to say and felt it was good for their students to hear. He felt he was making a small difference, and that the townspeople might be more inclined to help Jews in the future. The parents, of course, soon learned about this guest instructor, and word eventually reached the Nazis. The rabbi was arrested and tortured again about the whereabouts of his congregation. Refusing to cooperate, he was executed in the town square as an example of the fate that awaited Jews and those who sought to help them.

There is no record of how the rabbi felt about being tortured again and then led to his death. But we can imagine that he felt a sense of personal fulfillment as a rabbi, that first he sought to protect his congregation, despite being viciously tortured, and second, that he sought to combat the anti-Semitism that resulted in his own torture, and that led to the perilous threat to his congregation and the murder of so many of his fellow Jews. Perhaps he felt that something good came from his own suffering and from the plight that he found himself in; that he had turned straw into gold, in other words.

We can now ask the same theological questions we asked regarding the other two examples we have considered. He persevered. His mind stayed sharp. He was unwavering in protecting his people. He risked his own life in trying to make a dent against the evil of German contempt for the Jewish people. And where did all this come from, if not from the God he harbored within the depth of his being? And what did his actions reveal about this God, if not the mission of this God to promote even a small segment of goodness amidst the evil of hatred and murder?

The Photos We Need to See, for the God They Reveal

Here are the before and after photos of the woman who lost her face. Look how pretty she was, and look how hideous she became. How could she even venture out looking like that? But she did so much more. She gave talks and interviews. She was on national TV. Her face was on the cover of magazines. She was fiercely dedicated to making something of value from her own misfortune. The God within her was not to be silenced or defeated. While this is a startling example, the trials in our lives, while less disquieting, call out to the same God for the strength to bounce back and find some redeeming aspect in the suffering and torments that come with life.

Here are the before and after photos of her face:

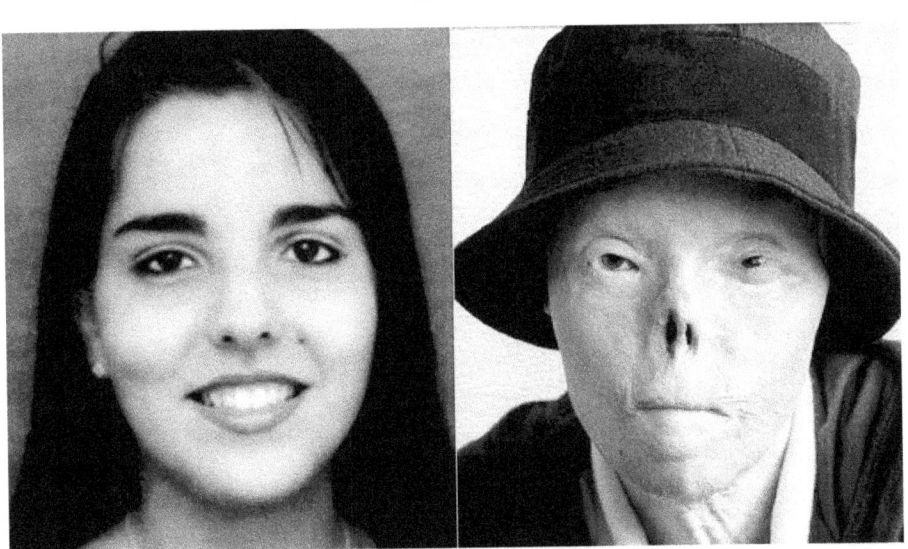

Bibliography

Adams, James. *The Republic of Plato*. Book V. Cambridge: Cambridge University Press, 1902.
Altizer, Thomas, and William Hamilton. *Radical Theology and the Death of God*. New York: Bobbs-Merrill, 1966.
Archer-Hind, Richard Dacre, ed., trans. *The Timaeus of Plato*. London: McMillan, 1888; reprinted Salem, NH: Ayers, 1988.
Armstrong, Karen. *The History of God*. New York: Ballantine, 1993.
Augustine. *Confessions*. Book III. Translated by Henry Chadwick. New York: Oxford University Press, 1991. Published as a World's Classic paperback, 1992.
Baron-Cohen, Simon. *The Science of Evil: On Empathy and Origins of Cruelty*. New York: Basic, 2011.
Bauchham, Richard. "Only a Suffering God Can Help: Divine Passibility in Modern Theology." *Themelios* 9 (1984) 6–12.
Barrow, John D. *The Origin of the Universe*. New York: Basic, 1994.
Becker, Ernest. *The Denial of Death*. New York: Free Press, 1997.
Bonhoeffer, Dietrich. *Letters and Papers from Prison*. London: SCM, 1967.
Borg, Marcus. *The God We Never Knew: Beyond Dogmatic Religion to a More Contemporary Faith*. San Francisco: HarperSanFrancisco, 1997.
Bostock, David. *Plato's Phaedo*. Oxford: Oxford University Press, 1986.
Braaten, Carl, and Robert W. Jenson. *A Map of Twentieth-Century Theology: Readings from Karl Barth to Radical Pluralism*. Minneapolis: Augsburg Fortress, 1955.
Brooks, Rodney Allen. *Fields of Color: The Theory That Escaped Einstein*. New Zealand: Rodney A. Brooks, 2014.
Bussey, Peter. *Signposts to God: How Modern Physics and Astronomy Point the Way to Belief*. Downers Grove: InterVarsity, 2016.
Camus, Albert. *The Myth of Sisyphus and Other Essays*. New York: Knopf, 1955.
Carroll, Sean. *The Big Picture: On the Origins of Life, Meaning, and the Universe Itself*. New York: Dutton, 2016.

Clayton, Philip, and Arthur Peacocke, eds. *In Whom We Live and Move and Have Our Being: Panentheistic Reflections on God's Presence in a Scientific World*. Grand Rapids: Eerdmans, 2004.

Clegg, Brian. *The God Effect: Quantum Entanglement, Science's Strangest Phenomenon*. New York: St. Martini's, 2009.

Collins, Graham. "Within Any Possible Universe, No Intellect Can Ever Know It All." *Scientific American*, March 2009. https://www.scientificamerican.com/article/limits-on-human-comprehension/.

Davies, Paul. *The Mind of God: The Scientific Basis for a Rational World*. New York: Touchstone, 1992.

Desbois, Patrick. *The Holocaust by Bullets: A Priest's Journey to Uncover the Truth behind the Murder of 1.5 Million Jews*. New York: Palgrave Macmillan, 2008.

Einstein, Albert. *Out of My Later Years*. New York: Citadel, 1956.

Flew, Anthony. *An Introduction to Western Philosophy: Ideas and Argument from Plato to Sarte*. New York: Thames and Hudson, 1971.

Ford, Dennis. *The Search for Meaning: A Short History*. Berkeley: University of California Press, 2007.

Ford, Lewis. "Divine Persuasion and the Triumph of the Good." *Christian Scholar* 50 (1967) 235–50.

Fuhrer, Markus. "Dietrich of Freiberg." *Stanford Encyclopedia of Philosophy*. February 23, 2005; revised May 24, 2019. https://plato.stanford.edu/entries/dietrich-freiberg/.

Galfard, Christophe. *The Universe in Your Hand: A Journey through Space, Time, and Beyond*. New York: Flatiron, 2016.

Gawande, Atul. *Being Mortal: Medicine and What Matters in the End*. New York: Metropolitan, 2014.

Gilkey, Langdon. *Naming the Whirlwind: The Renewal of God-Language*. Indianapolis: Bobbs-Merrill, 1969.

Gimbel, Stephen. "The Origin of Life," In *Redefining Reality: The Intellectual Implications of Modern Science*. Chantilly, VA: Teaching Company, 2015.

Goldstein, Rebecca Newberger. *36 Arguments for the Existence of God: A Work of Fiction*. New York: Vintage, 2010.

Grayling, A. C. "The Epoch of Human History." Chapter 2 of *The Age of Genius: The Seventeenth Century and the Birth of the Modern Mind*. New York: Bloomberg, 2016.

Greene, Brian. *The Elegant Universe: Superstrings, Hidden Dimensions, and the Quest for the Ultimate Theory*. New York: Vintage, 2000.

Halvorson, Hans, and Heige Kraph. "Cosmology and Theology." *Stanford Encyclopedia of Philosophy* . October 24, 2011; revised April 5, 2017. https://plato.stanford.edu/entries/cosmology-theology/.

Hartshorne, Charles. *The Divine Relativity: A Social Conception of God*. New Haven: Yale University Press, 1967.

Harris, James Franklin. *Analytic Philosophy of Religion*. Dordrecht, Netherlands: Springer, 2002.

Hawking, Stephen. *The Theory of Everything: The Origin and Fate of the Universe*. Beverly Hills, CA: Phoenix Books, 2005.

Hayes, Peter. *Why? Explaining the Holocaust*. New York: Norton, 2017.

Hazen, Robert. *The Story of Earth: The First 4.5 Billion Years, from Stardust to Living Planet*. New York: Penguin, 2013.
Held, Shai. *Abraham Joshua Heschel: The Call of Transcendence*. Indianapolis: Indiana University Press, 2013.
Isaacson, Walter. *Einstein: His Life and Universe*. New York: Simon and Schuster, 2007.
Jackson, Edgar Newman. *Coping with the Crises in Your Life*. Northvale, NJ: Aronson, 1986.
James, William. *The Varieties of Religious Experience: A Study in Human Nature*. United States: Seven Treasures, 2009.
Jammer, Max. *Einstein and Religion*. Princeton: Princeton University Press, 1999.
Jones, Serene. *Call It Grace: Finding Meaning in a Fractured World*. Station IV: Redeeming Life and Death. New York: Viking, 2019.
Karen, Robert. *Becoming Attached: Unfolding the Mystery of the Infant-Mother Bond and Its Impact on Later Life*. New York: Warner, 1977.
Kelsey, David. *The Fabric of Paul Tillich's Theology*. New Haven: Yale University Press, 1967.
Keverne, Barry. "Neurobiological and Molecular Approaches to Attachment and Bonding." In *Attachment and Bonding: A New Synthesis*, edited by Carol Sue Carter et al. Cambridge. Cambridge: MIT Press, 2005.
Kneier, Andrew. "God and Suffering." Chapter 7 of *Finding Your Way through Cancer*. Berkeley: Celestial Arts, 2010.
Kors, Alan Charles. *The Birth of the Modern Mind: The Intellectual History of the 17th and 18th Centuries*. Chantilly, VA: Teaching Company, 1998.
Laszlo, Ervin. *The Immortal Mind: Science and the Continuity of Consciousness Beyond the Brain*. With Anthony Peake. Rochester, VT: Inner Traditions, 2014.
Lear, Jonathan. "Death." Chapter 2 of *Happiness, Death, and the Remainder of Life*. Cambridge: Harvard University Press, 2000.
Lewis, Thomas, et al. *A General Theory of Love*. New York: Vintage, 2000.
Manning, Francis, and Katherine Zuzel. "Comparison of Types of Cell Death: Apoptosis and Necrosis." *Journal of Biological Education* 37 (2003) 141–45.
McFague, Sallie. "A Theology of Nature." Chapter 3 of *The Body of God: An Ecological Theology*. Minneapolis: Fortress, 1993.
Morgan, George, Jr. "Whitehead's Theory of Value." *International Journal of Ethics* 47 (1937) 308–16.
Niebuhr, Reinhold. *The Nature and Destiny of Man*. Vol. 1, *Human Nature*. New York: Scribner, 1964.
Nozick, Robert. "The Holocaust." In *The Examined Life: Philosophical Meditations*. New York: Simon & Schuster, 1989.
———. "Love's Bond." In *The Examined Life: Philosophical Meditations*. New York: Simon & Schuster, 1989.
Nuland, Sherwin. *How We Die: Reflections on Life's Final Chapter*. New York: Knopf, 1994.
Nussbaum, Martha. *Upheavals of Thought: The Intelligence of Emotions*. Cambridge: Cambridge University Press, 2003.
Padovano, Anthony. *The Estranged God*. New York: Sheed and Ward, 1966.
Pagels, Elaine. "God's Words or Human Words." Chapter 3 of *Beyond Belief: The Secret Gospel of Thomas*. New York: Random House, 2003.

Peters, Eugene. *The Creative Advance: An Introduction to Process Philosophy as a Context for Christian Faith*. St. Louis: Bethany, 1969.

Plato. "Phaedrus." In *Plato: Complete Works*, edited by John Cooper. Translated by Alexander Nehamas and Paul Woodruff. Indianapolis: Hackett, 1997.

———. "The Symposium." In *Plato: The Collected Dialogues*, edited by Edith Hamilton and Huntington Cairns. Translated by Michael Joyce. Princeton: Princeton University Press, 1961.

Polkinghorne, John. *Quarks, Chaos & Christianity*. London: Society for Promoting Christian Knowledge, Triangle, 1984.

Pollock, Steven. *Particle Physics for Non-physicists: A Tour of the Microcosmos*. Chantilly, VA. Teaching Company, 2003.

Prigogine, Ilya, and Isabelle Stengers. *Order out of Chaos: Man's Dialogue with Nature*. New York: Batam, 1984.

Principe, Lawrence M. *Science and Religion*. Chantilly, VA: Teaching Company, 2006.

Rahner, Karl, and Herbert Vorgrinler. "Divine Providence." In *Theological Dictionary*, edited by Cornelius Ernest, translated by Richard Strachan, 390. New York: Herder & Herder, 1967.

Randall, Lisa. *Knocking on Heaven's Door: How Physics and Scientific Thinking Illuminate the Universe and the Modern World*. New York: HarperCollins, 2011.

Rees, Martin. *Just Six Numbers: The Deep Forces That Shape the Universe*. New York: Basic, 2000.

Robinson, John A. T. *Honest to God*. Philadelphia: Westminster, 1963.

Rovelli, Carlo. *Seven Brief Lessons on Physics*. New York: Riverhead, 2016.

Salaman, Esther. *A Talk with Einstein*. Listener 54 (1955) 370–71.

Saltsman, Kirstie. "The Last Chapter: Cell Aging and Death." Chapter 5 of *Inside the Cell*. National Institute of Health publication no. 05-1051. [Bethesda, MD?]: US Department of Health and Human Services, National Institutes of Health, National Institute of General Medical Sciences, 2005.

Sartwell, Crispin. "Beauty." *Stanford Encyclopedia of Philosophy*. September 4, 2012; revised October 5, 2016. https://plato.stanford.edu/entries/beauty/.

Schleiermacher, Friedrich. *The Christian Faith*. Edinburgh: T. & T. Clark, 1928.

Seneca. *On the Shortness of Life: Life Is Long If You Know How to Use It*. New York: Penguin, 2005.

Silverman, Allan. "Plato's Middle Period Metaphysics and Epistemology." *Stanford Encyclopedia of Philosophy*. June 9, 2003; revised July 14, 2014. https://plato.stanford.edu/entries/plato-metaphysics/.

Singer, Irving. *The Nature of Love*. Vol. 1, *Plato to Luther*. Chicago: University of Chicago Press, 1984.

———. *The Nature of Love*. Vol. 2, *Courtly and Romantic*. Chicago: University of Chicago Press, 1984.

———. *The Nature of Love*. Vol. 3, *The Modern World*. Chicago: University of Chicago Press, 1989.

———. *Philosophy of Love: A Partial Summing-Up*. Cambridge: MIT Press, 2009.

Singh, Simon. *Big Bang: The Origin of the Universe*. New York: Harper Perennial, 2005.

Smith, T. V., ed. *From Thales to Plato: Philosophers Speak for Themselves*. Chicago: Phoenix Books, 1956.

Tegmark, Max. *Our Mathematical Universe: My Quest for the Ultimate Nature of Reality*. New York: Knopf, 2014.

Tillich, Paul. *The Courage to Be*. New Haven: Yale University Press, 1952.
———. "The Meaning of Joy." In *The New Being*, 141–51. New York: Scribner, 1955.
———. *The Shaking of the Foundations*. New York: Scribner, 1948.
———. *Systematic Theology*. Vol. 1. Chicago: University of Chicago Press, 1951.
Tooley, Michael. "The Problem of Evil." *Stanford Encyclopedia of Philosophy*. September 16, 2002; revised March 3, 2015. https://plato.stanford.edu/entries/evil/.
Weber, Bruce. "Life." *Stanford Encyclopedia of Philosophy*. August 15, 2003; revised November 7, 2011. https://plato.stanford.edu/entries/life/.
Werfel, John, et al. "Programed Death Is Favored by Natural Selection in Spatial Systems." *Physical Review Letters* 114 (2015) 1–5.
Whitehead, Alfred North. *Adventure of Ideas*. New York: Free Press, 1933.
———. *Process and Reality*. New York: Harper & Row, 1929.
———. *Religion in the Making*. Cleveland: World, 1926.
Williams, Bernard. "The Makropulos Case: Reflections on the Tedium of Immortality." In *Problems of the Self*, edited by Bernard Williams, 82–100. Cambridge: Cambridge University Press, 1973.
Wolpert, Lewis. *How We Live and Why We Die: The Secret Lives of Cells*. New York: Norton, 2011.
Zee, Anthony. *Fearful Symmetry: The Search for Beauty in Modern Physics*. New York: Macmillan, 1986.
———. *Quantum Field Theory in a Nutshell*. Princeton: Princeton University Press, 2010.

www.ingramcontent.com/pod-product-compliance
Lightning Source LLC
Chambersburg PA
CBHW051110160426
43193CB00010B/1384